# Holding the Line?
# The Effect of the
# Recent Border Build-up
# on Unauthorized
# Immigration

• • •

Belinda I. Reyes
Hans P. Johnson
Richard Van Swearingen

2002

PUBLIC POLICY INSTITUTE OF CALIFORNIA

Library of Congress Cataloging-in-Publication Data
Reyes, Belinda I., 1965-
   Holding the line? : the effect of the recent border build-up on
unauthorized immigration / Belinda I. Reyes, Hans P. Johnson,
Richard Van Swearingen.
     p.  cm.
   Includes bibliographical references.
   ISBN: 1-58213-059-0
   1. Illegal aliens—Government policy—United States. 2. Illegal
aliens—United States. 3. United States—Emigration and
immigration.  I. Johnson, Hans P. II. Van Swearingen, Richard,
1975– III. Title.

JV6483 .R474 2002
323.6'31'0973—dc21                                      2002072445

# Foreword

Anyone who has visited the San Diego-Tijuana border recently might well think that the Berlin Wall has been reconstructed in North America. The massive concrete wall, which etches the border into the desert landscape, is perhaps the best physical symbol of "prevention through deterrence," the current U.S. approach to controlling unauthorized immigration. There is little reliable evidence, however, that this policy, which now costs more than $2 billion annually, has significantly diminished such immigration.

PPIC research fellows Belinda Reyes and Hans Johnson, with the assistance of Richard Van Swearingen, set out in early 2000 to measure the effects of that policy on the flow of unauthorized immigrants to the United States. Their sources include INS and U.S. Census records, the Mexican 2000 Census, special surveys in Mexico, and focus groups in both California's Central Valley and Mexico. Those who had hoped that "prevention through deterrence" would turn the tide of undocumented flows will be discouraged by their findings. Increased border enforcement in the 1990s had little effect on the probability of migration from Mexico. Furthermore, the higher cost of crossing the border—in the form of both increased risk and the higher fees paid to smugglers— may induce unauthorized immigrants to stay longer in the United States than they did before the border enforcement build-up. The expanding U.S. economy and the increased durations of stay help to account for a large and rapidly growing population of unauthorized immigrants in the United States.

Some caution is necessary in interpreting these findings. First, no approach (or combination of approaches) has been especially successful at stopping unauthorized immigration. Beginning with the Bracero Program, which permitted guest workers from Mexico, the federal government has tried in various ways to balance the demands for both secure borders and low-wage immigrant labor. In 1986, Congress passed the Immigration Reform and Control Act, which granted amnesty to the unauthorized population residing in the United States at that time. Far from stopping the flow of undocumented immigrants, however, the measure led to an increase in that flow as family and other relations reunited in the United States—whether or not those relations were legal residents.

Second, border enforcement has always belonged to a set of domestic and international issues that is not easily subjected to the conventional political calculus. For example, U.S. employers have a long-standing interest in reliable supplies of low-wage immigrant labor, and Mexicans benefit significantly from remittances sent home by unauthorized workers in the United States. Other issues that feed the U.S. border enforcement policy include drug enforcement, national security, trade policy, and U.S.-Mexico relations. It is difficult to fashion an effective border strategy when key groups in both countries see real benefits to the continued flow of unauthorized workers across the border. In this sense, the wall on the San Diego-Tijuana border is one piece of a complex mosaic.

Third, economic cycles in both the United States and Mexico play a huge role in shaping the decision to immigrate without authorization. The income gradient between jobs in California and comparable ones in Mexico will continue to lead many young men and women in Mexico to undertake risky, expensive crossings—whether through the arid deserts of Arizona or in the stifling cargo trailers of an 18-wheel truck.

The authors conclude that a range of alternatives to current U.S. policy merit consideration. As they note, "A judicious combination of such policies could provide needed labor in the United States, protect workers' rights, reduce unauthorized immigration, and allow for a more accurate identification of legal residents." Such laudable objectives have been sought, in one form or another, for some 50 years. We trust that the findings from this most recent work by PPIC underscore the conclusion that no single policy effort is likely to achieve all of them.

David W. Lyon
President and CEO
Public Policy Institute of California

# Summary

Over the past two decades, immigration has become an important source of U.S. population growth and an increasingly contentious area of public policy. The recent terrorist attacks on the World Trade Center and the Pentagon have further increased appeals for restrictive immigration policy and stringent border controls. Well before the attacks, however, controlling the U.S.-Mexican border had become one of the primary objectives of federal immigration policy. Indeed, the Immigration and Naturalization Service (INS) budget for border enforcement increased sevenfold between 1980 and 1995 and then almost tripled between 1995 and 2001 (Figure S.1).[1] The sharp rise in border enforcement spending that began in the mid 1990s is attributable to a comprehensive, multiyear strategy crafted by the INS in 1994 with strong bipartisan support from the President and Congress.

The current border enforcement policy is based on the premise that apprehension deters illegal immigration. Acting on this premise in 1994, Attorney General Janet Reno and INS Commissioner Doris Meissner launched a nationwide strategy of "prevention-through-deterrence" first developed by Sylvester Reyes, then the Border Patrol Chief in El Paso. The multiyear strategy was designed to disrupt illegal immigration through traditional entry places along the Southwest border. Subsequently, the Illegal Immigration Reform and Immigrant Responsibility Act (IIRIRA) of 1996 substantially increased resources to prevent illegal immigration across the U.S.-Mexican border. The border enforcement strategy is designed to block entry through traditional routes and shift unauthorized traffic through remote areas, where the INS has a tactical advantage. To accomplish this goal, the INS has provided the Border Patrol with additional personnel, equipment, and

---

[1]Inflation-adjusted 2001 dollars.

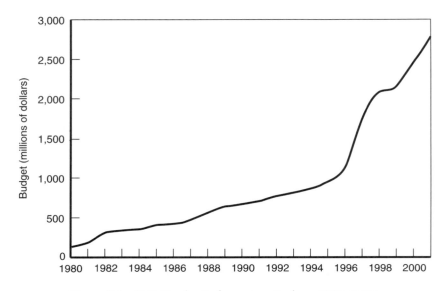

**Figure S.1—INS Border Enforcement Budget, 1980–2001**

technology to deter, detect, apprehend, and remove unauthorized immigrants.

Concerns about the policy's effectiveness are beginning to emerge among policymakers. It is not clear, for example, if the policy has led to a reduction in unauthorized immigration. In the report accompanying the House Budget Bill (H.R. 4690), the Appropriations Committee notes that the number of Border Patrol agents had increased 136 percent over the preceding four years and comments that "while the stream of illegal aliens may have slowed in the San Diego area, it has moved east to Arizona, New Mexico, and Texas."[2] Furthermore, a December 1997 General Accounting Office (GAO) report notes that "although developing a formal evaluation plan and implementing a rigorous and comprehensive evaluation of the [border] strategy may prove to be both difficult and potentially costly, without such an evaluation the Attorney General and Congress will have no way of knowing whether the billions

---

[2]House version of the FY 2001 Appropriations bill, which was passed June 14 by the House Appropriations Committee (H.R. 4690), and its corresponding committee report, House Report 106-680.

of dollars invested in reducing illegal immigration have produced the intended results."

## Research Goals and Approach

A complete evaluation of the recent build-up would analyze not only how it affects immigration but also how it is being implemented, how it affects border communities, how it affects drug trade and terrorism, and how it compares with other policy options. This report does not attempt to present a complete evaluation of the border enforcement strategy. Its narrower purpose is to examine the strategy's effectiveness at curbing unauthorized immigration and to investigate the ways in which the strategy has affected the behavior of potential and actual U.S.-bound migrants. Toward that end, it poses the following questions:

- Has increased border enforcement changed decisions to migrate to the United States?
- Has it altered the length of time immigrants stay in the United States?
- Has it decreased the number of unauthorized immigrants living in the United States?
- Has the build-up changed where and how people cross the U.S.-Mexican border?
- What has been the effect of increased enforcement on migrant deaths?
- What are other policy options to curb unauthorized immigration?

Answering these questions accurately is made especially difficult by the lack of complete and reliable data. In this report, we use many datasets, none of them perfect, to investigate the effect of border enforcement on immigration behavior.[3] Our focus is primarily, though not wholly, on unauthorized migration from Mexico, the leading source of unauthorized immigrants in the United States.

We use both descriptive and econometric techniques to determine the effects of the build-up on migration behavior. We examine time

---

[3]For complete descriptions of the data used in this report, see Appendix A.

trends to consider changes in migration and the number of immigrants in the United States before and after the border enforcement build-up. We explore the effect of the build-up on the decision to cross the U.S.-Mexican border—of new, repeat, and return migrants—independent of other factors. In particular, we develop models that control for migrants' networks, migration experience, household and community characteristics, and the economic conditions in both Mexico and the United States to isolate the effect of the border build-up on the probability of migration.[4]

## Key Findings

1. **There is no evidence that the border enforcement build-up as such has substantially reduced unauthorized border crossings.**

We find a decline in the probability of first-time migration in the latter part of the 1990s, as well as an increase in the probability of migration for experienced migrants during the same period. However, we do not find a statistically significant relationship between the build-up and the probability of migration. Economic opportunities in the United States and Mexico have a stronger effect on migration than does the number of agents at the border.

2. **There is strong evidence that unauthorized migrants are staying longer in the United States during the period of increased enforcement.**

The findings based on both the national data and the Mexican Migration Project (MMP)[5] sample indicate a decline in the probability of return in the 1990s. Analysis of the MMP sample shows no statistically significant effect of the build-up on the probability of return. But the national data indicate a continuing decline in the probability of return in the latter part of the 1990s, which could be the result of an increase in border

---

[4]Appendix B includes a complete description of all methods used in this report.

[5]The MMP is a survey of people and households living in primary sending regions in Mexico.

enforcement (see Figure S.2). Data from a 1992 survey in Mexico indicate that 20 percent of the people who moved to the United States 24 months prior to the survey year returned to Mexico within six months of migration. By 1997, this portion had declined to 15 percent. By the time of the Mexican 2000 Census, only 7 percent of those who moved 24 months prior to the census returned to Mexico within the first six months and only 11 percent had returned within a year.

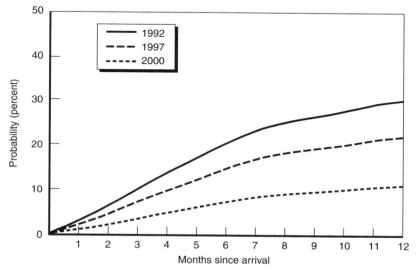

SOURCES: Authors' calculations from the 1992 and 1997 National Survey of Demographic Dynamics (ENADID) and the Mexican 2000 Census.

Figure S.2—Percent of Unauthorized Immigrants Who Return to Mexico Within One Year: 1992, 1997, and 2000

**3. The total number of unauthorized immigrants residing in the United States increased substantially during the mid to late 1990s.**

We find that the number of unauthorized immigrants residing in the United States is at an all-time high. Moreover, increases in the unauthorized population residing in the United States in the 1990s appear to be very large (see Figure S.3). The total population of

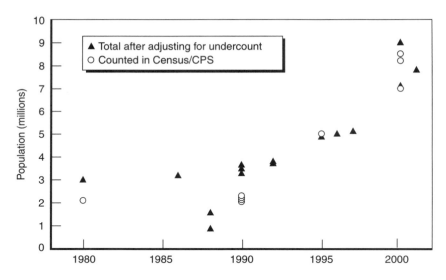

**Figure S.3—Estimates of the Number of Unauthorized Immigrants in the United States, 1980–2001**

unauthorized residents in 2000 is estimated to be at least 7 million and perhaps as many as 9 million people.

Although estimates of the annual flow of unauthorized immigrants are uncertain, they seem to indicate that flows into the United States were very high during the period immediately after passage of the Immigration Reform and Control Act (IRCA) (the late 1980s and 1990), they declined with the recession of the early 1990s, and they increased substantially in the very late 1990s. Moreover, the number of unauthorized farm workers increased substantially during the period of increased border enforcement. Overall, the picture is one of a large and rapidly growing population of unauthorized immigrants in the United States.

**4. The border enforcement strategy has achieved some of its goals. In particular, it increased the probability of apprehension, changed the crossing places of migrants, and increased the costs associated with crossing the U.S.-Mexican border.**

Immigrants are now taking alternative routes across the U.S.-Mexican border, and there has been an increase in the probability of apprehension (see Figure S.4). However, the number of apprehensions did not decline substantially until 2001. It is unclear whether this decline was due to increased border enforcement or to a deterioration of the U.S. economy and the attacks of September 11. An unintended, though predictable, consequence of heightened enforcement during this period was the increase in both the use of smugglers and the smugglers' fees.

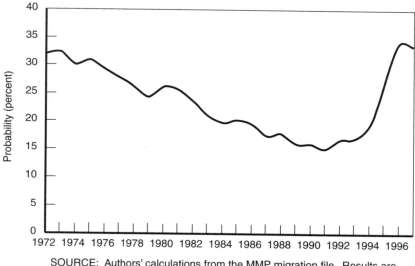

SOURCE: Authors' calculations from the MMP migration file. Results are presented as three-year moving averages.

Figure S.4—Probability of Apprehension, Male Household Heads

**5. During the period of increased enforcement, the number of unauthorized migrants who died while attempting to cross the border has increased.**

Another unintended consequence of the border strategy has been an increase in the number of migrants dying while crossing the border (see Figure S.5). This number appears to decline in the late 1980s and early 1990s, reaching a low point in the years immediately preceding the

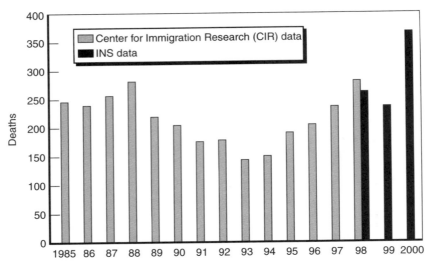

Figure S.5—Reported Migrant Deaths

increase in border enforcement. Following the introduction of the Border Patrol's strategy, however, migrant deaths increased rapidly, reaching a 15-year peak in fiscal year (FY) 2000.

Unauthorized migrants are also more likely to die from environmental causes now than ever before. In FY 2000, the Border Patrol recorded 135 deaths from exposure to heat and 92 deaths from drowning; in 1994, the Border Patrol recorded only nine exposure deaths and 48 drownings. The shift in causes of death appears to be due to changes in crossing locations.

## Conclusions for the Current Policy Debate

Despite large increases in spending and Border Patrol resources over the past nine years, the number of unauthorized immigrants in the United States has increased to levels higher than those in the pre-IRCA period. Although the border build-up has achieved some of its goals, it may have produced some unintended consequences as well. Migrants who successfully cross the border stay longer in the United States than they did in the past. There has been an increase in the number of deaths at the border, and the increased use of hired guides, or coyotes, may have expanded the very profitable human smuggling industry.

Reducing unauthorized immigration to the United States is a very complex task, one that requires a multitude of policy tradeoffs. This report does not advocate a specific set of policies; rather, it presents current alternatives to controlling and identifying the flow of unauthorized immigrants, including internal enforcement efforts, employer sanctions, national ID cards, regularization, guest-worker programs, and foreign direct investment. No single policy is able to address all facets of unauthorized immigration. But a combination of policies could provide needed labor, protect workers' rights, reduce unauthorized immigration, and allow for more accurate identification of legal residents of the United States.

# Contents

# Figures

# Tables

# Acknowledgments

We are grateful to many people who helped us develop this report. In particular, Deborah Reed generously shared her time and guidance at every step of this process. We would also like to recognize our group of research associates, consultants, and interviewers, who put into action our vision and provided us with their expertise. Research associates Joe Hayes and Amanda Bailey provided invaluable assistance. Victoria Robinson and Rafael Alarcón were our consultants for the focus groups and the survey. Anna García, Luz Torres, Macrina Alarcón, Olivia Cuevas, and Socorro Torres Sarmiento were our "dream team" of interviewers, who taught us how to conduct a survey and shared their passion for talking to people. Norma Herrera and Diego Valencia did an exceptional job transcribing and translating our qualitative data.

We are grateful to Abel Valenzuela, Jeffrey Ponting, Rufino Domínguez, Oralia Maced, Leon Sebástias, Irma Luna, and the staffs of the day labor site in Hollywood, the day labor site in West Los Angeles, and the Domestic Workers Group for their assistance in organizing the focus groups. They served as our entry into the sites and made people comfortable enough to talk with us about their experiences, bringing immigrants' voices into our report. We are most grateful to the migrants we spoke to in Fresno, Madera, and Los Angeles, as well as the people of Chavinda, who welcomed us into their homes without hesitation.

Our advisory group—Andres Jimenez, Frank D. Bean, Wayne Cornelius, Rodolfo Cruz, Katharine Donato, Jorge Durand, Manuel García y Griego, Susan Martin, Philip Martin, Jeff Passel, Georges Vernez, Robert Warren, and Karen Woodrow-Lafield—gave generously of their time and expertise.

Last but not least, we want to acknowledge our reviewers, Mark Baldassare, Peter Richardson, Jeff Passel, Laura Hill, and Karen Woodrow-Lafield, and our copyeditors at RAND. They painstakingly read and commented on this report and contributed enormously to its improvement and completion. Any remaining mistakes are those of the authors.

# 1. Introduction

Faced with a severe economic recession and growing political pressure to reduce the number of unauthorized immigrants, Congress and the Clinton Administration in 1994 launched one of the most ambitious border enforcement efforts in U.S. history. The goal was to prevent illegal entry rather than to apprehend illegal aliens once they entered the United States, as was the previous Border Patrol policy (Cornelius, 2001). Modeled after the strategy pioneered by former El Paso Border Patrol Chief Sylvester Reyes, the policy called for increasing the number of Border Patrol agents, installing multiple physical barriers, and using enhanced electronic surveillance equipment and other measures to make it more difficult for illegal immigrants to enter (Cornelius, 1997; General Accounting Office (GAO), 1997a). In that same year, Congress authorized 1,000 additional Border Patrol agents every year from 1995 to 2001 (Gimpel and Edwards, 1999; GAO, 1999a,b).

The policy also called for increasing enforcement efforts at traditional urban crossing locations, securing those sectors, and then focusing resources at sectors where crossings have become more common (GAO, 1997a, Cornelius, 1997). In September 1993, the Immigration and Naturalization Service (INS) began Operation Hold-the-Line in El Paso, Texas; in October 1994, it launched Operation Gatekeeper in San Diego and Operation Safeguard in Arizona; and in August 1997, it initiated Operation Rio Grande in the McAllen sector (see Figure 1.1). Under the second phase of the border strategy, the INS increased the number of Border Patrol agents in Tucson, Del Rio, and Laredo. Now in Phase III, the INS is deploying agents to El Centro, Yuma, and Marfa (GAO, 1999b).

In 1997, President Clinton signed into law the Illegal Immigration Reform and Immigrant Responsibility Act (IIRIRA), which significantly increased the number of Border Patrol agents and technological resources

Spokane
Blaine
Havre
Livermore
Grand Forks
Detroit
Buffalo
Swanton
Houlton
San Diego
El Centro
Yuma
Tucson
El Paso
Marfa
Del
Rio
New Orleans
Miami
Headquarters,
Border Patrol
Laredo
McAllen
Ramey

SOURCE: INS website.

**Figure 1.1—Border Patrol Sectors**

to prevent illegal immigration. For example, it provided for the use of aircraft, helicopters, night-vision equipment, sensors, computer systems, and four-wheel-drive vehicles. IIRIRA also allocated millions of dollars for the construction of a triple fence along some portions of the U.S.- Mexican border. In addition to adding resources and physical barriers, IIRIRA stiffened civil and criminal penalties for illegal entry and assisting illegal entry. It also authorized the use of wiretaps for the investigation of alien smuggling and document fraud (Espenshade, Baraka, and Huber, 1997).

## Evaluating the Border Build-up

The GAO has published a number of reports evaluating the INS border enforcement strategy,[1] and it has found that some of the intended

---

[1]The GAO has conducted six studies of border control in the United States in the past 10 years: *Border Patrol: Southwest Border Enforcement Affected by Mission Expansion and Budgets*, GAO/T-GGD-72BE, March 28, 1991; *Immigration Enforcement: Problems in Controlling the Flow of Illegal Aliens*, GAO/GGD-93-39, June 30, 1993; *Border Control: Revised Strategy Is Showing Some Positive Results*, GAO/GGD-95-30, December 29, 1994; *Staffing and Enforcement Activities*, GAO/GGD-96-65, March 11, 1996; *Illegal*

goals of the policy have been achieved: People are moving from the traditional high-activity entry points such as San Diego and El Paso to other locations along the border; more people appear to be using fraudulent documents; and the prices charged by smugglers have gone up, indicating an increase in the difficulty of crossing (GAO, 1999b). However, the reports make clear that an overall evaluation of the policy's effectiveness in deterring illegal entry cannot be made with the data available. Only such an evaluation can determine whether the billions of dollars invested in the strategy are producing the intended results (GAO, 1997a, 1999b).

A careful evaluation of El Paso's operation found that the policy has been effective at reducing the crossing of certain "local" illegal crossers— domestic-service workers and street vendors who live in Ciudad Juarez and cross daily to work in El Paso—but it has had no deterrent effect on long-distance crossers (Bean et al., 1994). In an examination of Operation Gatekeeper, Cornelius (1997) found that the operation has forced illegal crossers into other areas but has not reduced the overall flow. Cornelius (2001) also argues that the build-up has led to an increase in the number of migrant deaths.

As the risk and cost of crossing the border have increased, border enforcement has also had a number of unintended effects. Some researchers argue that it may be leading to a lengthening of the immigrant stay (Kossoudji, 1992; Espenshade, Baraka, and Huber, 1997; Massey, Durand, and Malone, 2002; Reyes, 2001). Others argue that an increase in enforcement may lead to more migration, as prospective migrants fear further enforcement and cross before doing so becomes more difficult (Massey and Espinosa, 1997). Still others argue that an increase in enforcement may lead to an increase in the likelihood of a second trip, decreasing the number of years or months people live in Mexico, as they try to return to the United States as quickly as possible (Kossoudji, 1992).

Other researchers have found that the effect of past increases in enforcement on the probability of apprehension is small (Crane et al.,

*Immigration: Southwest Border Strategy Results Inconclusive; More Evaluation Needed,* GAO/GGD-98-21, December 11, 1997; and *Illegal Immigration: Status for Southwest Border Strategy Implementation,* GAO/GGD-99-44, May 19, 1999.

1990; Donato, Durand, and Massey, 1992; Espenshade, 1990; Heyman, 1995; Massey and Singer, 1995; Singer and Massey, 1998). This research, however, does not directly examine the effect of border enforcement on migration behavior, nor does it examine the most recent period of the greatest increase in enforcement.

## Unanswered Questions

Using the most recent data available, this report attempts to answer several questions left unanswered by previous research. A combination of data sources are used to evaluate the effects of increased border enforcement on migration behavior. These effects include changes in

- The probability of making a trip illegally to the United States as a first-time migrant,
- The likelihood of remigration,
- The duration of stay in the United States,
- The number of unauthorized immigrants living in the United States,
- Preferred routes and crossing methods, and
- Migrant deaths.

The premise of the build-up is that an increase in border enforcement will lead to a reduction in the number of unauthorized immigrants entering the United States and hence to a decline in the number of immigrants in the United States at any one time (GAO, 1997a). The issue, however, is not only whether the build-up reduces the number of persons attempting to cross but whether potential immigrants choose to move now, later, or not at all. The deterrent effect of an increase in enforcement might be quite small if it only leads some immigrants to delay their migration temporarily to save enough money to cover the higher migration costs. A related issue is the length of time those who migrate stay in the United States. Greater enforcement might have the perverse effect of increasing stays in the United States and increasing the likelihood of permanent settlement. Longer stays allow successful crossers to recoup the higher costs of crossing and to avoid the increased likelihood of apprehension associated with multiple return crossings. The success of the enforcement build-up thus depends on the magnitude and direction of its effects on these different types of migratory responses.

This report addresses these questions as follows. Chapter 2 looks at the effect of the recent enforcement build-up on the probability of migration for first-time and experienced migrants. Chapter 3 explores the effects of current enforcement efforts on the length of time migrants spend in the United States. Chapter 4 provides estimates of the total number of unauthorized immigrants living in the United States at any one point in time and the number of unauthorized immigrants entering the United States. Chapter 5 looks for evidence of changes in the manner of crossing, crossing places, probability of apprehension, and the use of smugglers (coyotes) that could have resulted from the border build-up. Chapter 6 describes trends in the causes, places, and likelihood of death among unauthorized migrants. Finally, Chapter 7 discusses the advantages and disadvantages of different policy options aimed at reducing unauthorized immigration.

# 2. Has Increased Border Enforcement Changed the Decision to Immigrate?

Increases in border enforcement are intended not only to increase the difficulty of border crossings but also to deter potential migrants from choosing to migrate in the first place. In this chapter, we explore this deterrent effect of the border build-up by modeling an unauthorized immigrant's decision to migrate to the United States from Mexico. Temporal changes in the probability of migrating to the United States could be the result of increases in border enforcement, but they also might be attributable to other factors, such as economic conditions in the United States and Mexico. We use statistical models to identify the distinct effect of increased border enforcement apart from other factors. The analysis uses data from the Mexican Migration Project (MMP), the Mexican 2000 Census, and the 1992 and 1997 National Survey of Demographic Dynamics (ENADID).[1]

We examine the migration of first-time migrants separately from that of experienced migrants, as the border build-up may have had a smaller effect on experienced migrants, who have information or skills that could help them overcome the obstacles of border enforcement. Inexperienced migrants from regions with a long history of migration may also be less affected by the build-up than are those from new sending regions. We therefore analyze a subsample of communities to determine the effect of the build-up on inexperienced migrants from nontraditional sending regions in Mexico.[2]

---

[1] For details on the data, see Appendix A. For a discussion of methodology, see Appendix B.

[2] The most recent MMP surveys disproportionately sample new sending regions. They are in the states of Zacatecas (7.6 percent), Guerrero (9.8 percent), San Luis Potosi

We find a decline in the probability of migration for first-time migrants in the latter part of the 1990s and an increase in the probability of migration of experienced migrants. However, we do not find a statistically significant relationship between the build-up and the probability of migration. Economic opportunities in the United States and Mexico and the migrants' social networks appear to have a stronger effect on migration than does the number of agents along the U.S.-Mexican border.

## Effect of the Build-up on the Decision to Migrate: New Migrants

Figure 2.1 shows the probability that a person with no prior migration experience will move to the United States, controlling for changes in personal, household, and community characteristics over time.[3] The probability of making an unauthorized move to the United States increased for both men and women from 1982 until 1989. Previous researchers also found an increase in unauthorized immigration in the 1980s, especially after passage of the Immigration Reform and Control Act (IRCA); such immigration declined during the recession of the early 1990s (Johnson, 1996; Warren, 2000). For men, the probability of migration declined substantially in 1991, for the first time in 10 years. That probability remained below IRCA levels until the economic crisis of the mid 1990s in Mexico, which led to the devaluation of the peso in 1995. By 1997, migration probabilities had

---

(12.5 percent), Oaxaca (11.8 percent), Sinaloa (11 percent), Puebla (11.9 percent), Guanajuato (4.6 percent), Jalisco (7.6 percent), Baja California Norte (11.8 percent), Colima (4.53 percent), and Aguas Calientes (6.8 percent).

[3]In this model, we control for age, education, headship status, the migration experience of other household members (as measured by having a family member who entered the United States during the previous 10 years), and whether or not someone in the same household has been legalized. We also try to control for family resources by including a variable for owning a home or land. We hold constant for community characteristics (whether the sending community is small, medium, or large; the proportion of men employed in agriculture; and a dummy for Mexican state). The results for the models are presented in Appendix B.

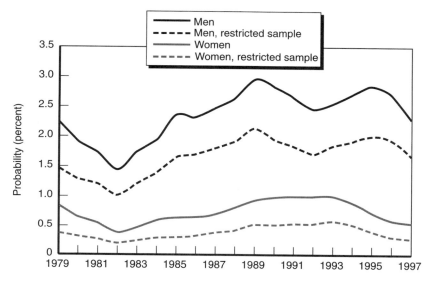

SOURCE: Authors' calculations from the MMP. Results are presented as three-year moving averages.

NOTES: The restricted sample comprises communities surveyed after 1994.

Figure 2.1—Probability of Moving Illegally to the United States by the Age of 20[4]

declined to pre-IRCA levels.[5] For women, the probability of migration increased until 1989 and remained at around 1 percent until 1994. But, coinciding with the beginning of increased enforcement, the probability of migration declined in the latter part of the 1990s.[6]

Although we observe changes in migration probabilities in Figure 2.1, it is impossible to determine what the probabilities of migration would have been without the enforcement build-up. To better understand what drives these migration decisions, we consider two other

---

[4]In order to do this simulation, we set age equal to 20 and estimated the probability of migration using the mean of all the other variables in the model and their beta coefficients.

[5]The probability of migration in these years is significantly different from that in 1989. We also conducted tests of the significance of the difference from one year to the next. For the most part, the pattern was significant at a 5 percent level.

[6]For the most part, the year differences are statistically significant at a 5 percent level.

factors: U.S. immigration policy and the conditions of the Mexican and U.S. economies.[7]

The findings in Table 2.1 show no statistically significant effect of the U.S. border enforcement build-up on unauthorized Mexican immigration. Even before controlling for changes in the sample (the first and fourth columns of Table 2.1),[8] the build-up appears to have had no effect on migration probabilities through 1998.[9] The coefficient on line watch hours is positive, indicating that an increase in enforcement would lead to an increase in the probability of migration; however, the effect could be temporary, as seen by the negative coefficient in the squared term. This pattern would indicate that as the number of agents increases, a turnaround point at which migration decreases with increases in enforcement is possible. However, both coefficients are statistically insignificant.

The trends we observe appear to be related to factors other than increases in enforcement. The most important factors include the economic conditions in the United States and Mexico, IRCA, and immigrant networks. Economic conditions in both Mexico and the United States have a stronger effect on the probability of migration than does the build-up at the border.[10] Men and women are less likely to move to the United States when the U.S. unemployment rate is increasing. In 1998, the unemployment rate was 4.7 percent. A 10 percent increase, to 5.1 percent, decreases the probability of migration by

---

[7]These models explore the effect of macro conditions on the time trend after controlling for changes in the characteristics of migrants, their households, and their communities. We run a two-stage model in which we first look at the effect of personal, household, and community characteristics on the time trend. We then explore the effect of macro conditions on the unexplained time trend. See Appendix B for details.

[8]The table shows results for three different models: the raw effect of macro conditions before we control for changes in the characteristics of the sample; the effect of macro factors once we have controlled for changes in the sample; and the effect on a restricted sample of communities surveyed after 1994, in which new sending regions are oversampled.

[9]Either the build-up had no effect on the probability of migration or the effect was too small and much less important than other factors as of 1998.

[10]A well-known finding in the literature is the importance of economic factors in the decision to migrate. For example, see Massey and Espinosa (1997); Massey et al. (1987).

Table 2.1

Parameter Estimates for Variables in the Second-Stage OLS Equation:  Model of the Probability of First Migration[11]

| | Men | | | Women | | |
|---|---|---|---|---|---|---|
| | No Controls | With Controls | Restricted Sample | No Controls | With Controls | Restricted Sample |
| Intercept | −1.15*** | −1.57*** | −2.4*** | −2.2*** | −1.65** | −3.1*** |
| | (0.42) | (0.414) | (0.38) | (0.66) | (0.66) | (0.95) |
| Conditions of the Mexican economy | | | | | | |
| Mexican GDP per | 0.04 | 0.04 | 0.04 | 0.06 | 0.05 | 0.058 |
| capita | (0.03) | (0.029) | (0.026) | (0.046) | (0.05) | (0.066) |
| Mexican GDP squared | −0.0009* | −0.0009* | −0.001** | −0.001 | −0.0009 | −0.001 |
| | (0.0005) | (0.0005) | (0.0004) | (0.0007) | (0.0007) | (0.001) |
| Exchange rate | −0.03 | −0.023 | −0.05 | −0.11 | −0.09 | −0.136 |
| | (0.059) | (0.058) | (0.05) | (0.092) | (0.09) | (0.123) |
| Conditions of the U.S. economy | | | | | | |
| U.S. unemployment | −0.13** | −0.129** | −0.11** | −0.16** | −0.16* | −0.125 |
| rate | (0.05) | (0.049) | (0.045) | (0.078) | (0.078) | (0.112) |
| U.S. immigration policy | | | | | | |
| Legal admissions | 0.28** | 0.30** | 0.41*** | 0.35* | 0.33 | 0.378 |
| | (0.122) | (0.12) | (0.11) | (0.19) | (0.192) | (0.269) |
| Legal admissions | −0.01** | −0.012** | −0.017*** | −0.013 | −0.012 | −0.014 |
| squared | (0.005) | (0.006) | (0.005) | (0.009) | (0.008) | (0.011) |
| Line watch hours | 0.17 | 0.24 | 0.353 | 0.46 | 0.24 | 0.654 |
| | (0.34) | (0.33) | (0.28) | (0.535) | (0.53) | (0.746) |
| Line watch hours | −0.04 | −0.03 | −0.039 | −0.07 | −0.033 | −0.065 |
| squared | (0.04) | (0.039) | (0.033) | (0.063) | (0.06) | (0.083) |
| $R^2$ | 67.5% | 73.8% | 83.5% | 66% | 57.1% | 56.2% |
| Adjusted R | 54.5% | 63.3% | 46.9% | 52.3% | 40% | .38.7% |

NOTES:  **** = significant at a 1 percent level; *** = significant at a 5 percent level; ** = significant at a 10 percent level.

---

[11]The independent variables in these models were normalized.  Line watch hours is normalized at 1 million hours, legal admissions at 100,000 people, and gross domestic product (GDP) per capita at 100 pesos.  During this period of the analysis, the average GDP per capita in Mexico was 2,643 pesos, 700,000 people were legally admitted to the United States per year, the unemployment rate in the United States was 6.7 percent, and the INS spent on average 2.6 million man-hours guarding the U.S.-Mexican border.

0.2 percent. Although the change appears to be small, its effect could be large. In 1998, for example, the population in the MMP states was nearly 43 million people, with 16 million males between the ages of 16 and 35. Holding other factors constant, our estimates indicate that a 10 percent increase in the U.S. unemployment rate will discourage 28,800 males from crossing illegally to the United States.

The conditions of the Mexican economy also affect the probability of men migrating. As found in previous research, men are more likely to leave Mexico when the GDP is higher, but the effect decreases as the GDP increases (Massey et al., 1987; Massey and Espinosa, 1997; Portes and Bach, 1985). The combined effect leads to a decline in the probability of migration as the Mexican economy grows. In 1998, the GDP per capita in Mexico was 4,400 pesos. A 10 percent increase in the per capita GDP would decrease the probability of migration for men by 0.5 percent. As there are close to 16 million males between 16 and 35 in the MMP states, this increase alone would discourage 78,400 men from migrating illegally to the United States.

To capture the effect of IRCA on migration probabilities, we look at changes in legal admissions in the United States, and we find that IRCA had a strong effect on the probability of migration. However, it had no statistically significant effect on women's migration behavior once we control for changes in the characteristics of the sample.[12] Similar to the findings in previous research (Johnson, 1996; Warren, 2000), we find an increase in illegal immigration during the IRCA period, even among new sending regions, as shown in the third column of Table 2.1. There is, however, a turnaround point at which an increase in legal immigration would lead to less unauthorized immigration.[13] In 1998, almost

---

[12]The effect of IRCA could be operating indirectly for women, since increasing the number of legal migrants in Mexican households increases migration probabilities. In another model, we looked at the effect of having a legal migrant in the household over time by including interactions in the model, and we found that people were more likely to move illegally if they had a family member who had been legalized. But their probability of migration declined during the enforcement period. As the build-up made it more difficult to cross the border, it is possible that people increasingly preferred to wait to legalize their status rather than crossing illegally.

[13]The opposite is also true: A decline in legal immigration at some point would lead to an increase in illegal immigration.

660,000 people were granted legal permanent status. Our estimates indicate that a 10 percent increase in legal admissions would lead to a 0.3 percent increase in unauthorized male immigrants—an additional 44,800 new male migrants.

Finally, originating from a household with other migrants and having a legal migrant in the home increases the probability of migration, especially for women. Changes in both the number of migrants and the legalization status of many unauthorized immigrants as a result of IRCA would therefore increase the probability of migration of other household members. For further discussion of these results, see Appendix B.

In sum, we find a decline in the probability of first-time migration for both men and women during the last years of the 1990s, but this effect is statistically unrelated to the number of hours spent guarding the U.S.-Mexican border. It is possible that a further increase in the number of agents at the border would lead to a decline in the probability of migration; however, that number may need to be increased substantially to produce this effect. Our research indicates that both the economic conditions in the United States and Mexico and the networks and resources available to households in Mexico are more important than increased border enforcement in explaining first-time migration to the United States.

## Effect of the Build-up on the Decision to Migrate: Experienced Migrants[14]

Next, we look at the change in the likelihood of migration before and after the build-up for those with previous migration experience. Some experienced migrants may choose to move more quickly to the United States because they fear the difficulty of crossing may increase with time (Massey and Espinosa, 1997). Others, however, when faced

---

[14]In this section, we look at the probability of making a second trip to the United States as an unauthorized immigrant. We restricted the sample to migrants who made one or two trips to the United States and looked at the number of years it took them to make the second trip. Although we limited the analysis to one or two moves, the findings are generally applicable because 84 percent of the unauthorized immigrants in the sample moved once or twice.

with the increased costs and risks of crossing associated with heightened enforcement, may decide to stay in Mexico.

The likelihood of remigration appears to have increased during the peak enforcement years, especially for male migrants (Figure 2.2).[15] Although only about 5 percent of the men who returned to Mexico made a second trip to the United States within the first year in 1984, close to 11 percent made a second trip within the first year in 1997. The results for women are less precise due to sample size limitations, but they also exhibit similar trends.[16] The increase in the probability of remigration

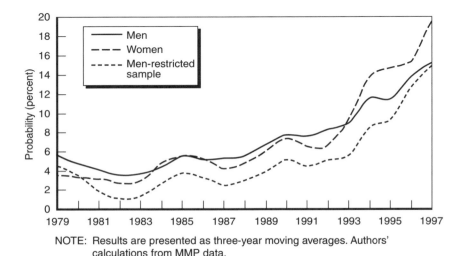

NOTE: Results are presented as three-year moving averages. Authors' calculations from MMP data.

**Figure 2.2—Probability of Remigration Within One Year After Return**

---

[15]This figure shows the probability of migration within one year after returning to Mexico, after controlling for changes in the characteristics of the sample, migrants' experience in the United States in their first trip, their household resources, and the characteristics of their communities of origin. The results of the full model are presented in Appendix B.

[16]For men, the results for 1980 to 1984, 1987, and 1994 to 1998 are statistically significant and show an increasing probability of remigration. For women, the results for 1982, 1994, 1995, 1997, and 1998 are statistically significant at a 5 percent level. They also show an increase in the probability of remigration over time. The sample size in the restricted model is too small to generate any significant coefficient in the time trend for women.

during the period of stepped-up enforcement runs counter to INS expectations.

We explored the effect of economic opportunities in Mexico and the United States, as well U.S. immigration policy, on the probability of remigration (Table 2.2).[17] The only variable that consistently matters for experienced migrants is the level of unemployment in the United States. An increase in the unemployment rate in the United States leads to a decline in their probability of migration.

Overall, the relationship between line watch hours and the probability of migration is statistically insignificant. That is, the border build-up appears to have no effect on the probability of migration for experienced migrants, or the effect is too small to be captured in this model. The build-up does, however, have a positive and significant effect on the probability of remigration of male migrants in the restricted sample of new sending regions. At least in the short term, the build-up appears to accelerate migration for experienced migrants in new sending regions in Mexico, perhaps due to a fear of increasing difficulty in crossing (Massey and Espinosa, 1997).[18]

In addition to the conditions of the U.S. economy, the social and economic conditions in Mexico also affect remigration (see results in Appendix B). The unauthorized immigrant's state of origin, the type of job he or she held in the United States in the first trip, and his or her destination in the United States all play an important part in determining whether or not a migrant will make an additional trip to the United States.

To summarize, the probability of remigration has been increasing over time, and there is no evidence that increased enforcement had lowered this probability as of 1998. Unauthorized Mexican immigrants with previous migration experience were substantially more likely to make a second trip to the United States during the enforcement build-up than they were before the build-up. Also, it is possible that the build-up

---

[17]These are the results of a second-stage model. Although better than a single-stage model, this approach has its limitations. See Appendix B for discussion.

[18]This could also be the result of the way communities are selected in the MMP sample. It is possible that these regions were chosen because they experienced increases in migration during the 1990s due to factors other than the build-up.

## Table 2.2

### Parameter Estimates for Variables in the Second-Stage OLS Equation: Model of Remigration[19]

| | Men | | | Women | | |
|---|---|---|---|---|---|---|
| | No Controls | With Controls | Restricted Sample | No Controls | With Controls | Restricted Sample |
| Intercept | −0.98 | −0.41 | −6.18 | −0.127 | −5.7 | −22.2** |
| | (0.60) | (0.65) | (7.4) | (0.83) | (3.7) | (8.39) |
| **Conditions of Mexican economy** | | | | | | |
| Mexican GDP per capita | −0.00009 | −0.015 | 0.14 | −0.01 | 0.03 | −0.27 |
| | (0.04) | (0.04) | (0.46) | (0.05) | (0.23) | (0.52) |
| Mexican GDP squared | −0.00002 | 0.0003 | −0.002 | 0.0002 | −0.0003 | 0.003 |
| | (0.0006) | (0.0007) | (0.0006) | (0.0007) | (0.003) | (0.008) |
| Exchange rate | −0.01 | −0.018 | −0.05 | −0.07 | −0.2 | −0.299 |
| | (0.07) | (0.08) | (0.05) | (0.095) | (0.42) | (0.91) |
| **Conditions of U.S. economy** | | | | | | |
| U.S. unemployment rate | −0.13* | −0.129* | −1.21 | −0.25*** | −0.05 | −0.44 |
| | (0.06) | (0.069) | (0.78) | (0.08) | (0.37) | (0.91) |
| **U.S. immigration policy** | | | | | | |
| Legal admissions | 0.16 | 0.10 | −1.03 | 0.24 | 0.04 | 3.16 |
| | (0.155) | (0.17) | (1.73) | (0.18) | (0.88) | (1.98) |
| Legal admissions squared | −0.007 | −0.003 | 0.05 | −0.008 | −0.0003 | −0.12 |
| | (0.007) | (0.007) | (0.07) | (0.008) | (0.04) | (0.08) |
| Line watch hours | 0.55 | 0.38 | 8.94* | 0.41 | 2.8 | 5.99 |
| | (0.44) | (0.47) | (4.99) | (0.57) | (2.5) | (5.6) |
| Line watch hours squared | −0.06 | −0.02 | −0.84 | −0.04 | −0.24 | −0.49 |
| | (0.05) | (0.054) | (0.53) | (0.06) | (0.29) | (0.60) |
| $R^2$ | 65% | 71% | 34.4% | 63.1% | 28.3% | 57.9% |
| Adjusted R | 50% | 69.4% | 8.2% | 48.4% | −0.4% | 41% |

NOTES: **** = significant at a 1 percent level; *** = significant at a 5 percent level; ** = significant at a 10 percent level. The first model has only year dummies. The second model controls for personal, family, and community characteristics. The third model looks at only those communities surveyed after 1994. The sample sizes for women are small, leading to less-significant results.

---

[19]During this period of the analysis, the average GDP per capita in Mexico was 2,643 pesos, 700,000 people per year were admitted legally or changed status, the unemployment rate in the United States was 6.7 percent, and the INS spent on average 2.6 million man-hours guarding the U.S.-Mexican border. The GDP is normalized to 100 pesos, the legal admissions to 100,000, and the number of hours to 1 million.

escalated this pattern, at least for new sending regions. As is the case for first-time migrants, the conditions of the U.S. economy are one of the strongest predictors of remigration.

## Effect of the Build-up on the Decision to Migrate: All Migrants

To get a more recent picture of the changes and to confirm the patterns observed in the MMP data, we look at the Mexican 2000 Census and the 1992 and 1997 ENADID. Both are nationally representative samples of Mexican households that capture migration five years prior to the survey year for usual household members of each Mexican household.[20] With these samples, we are able to explore changes in migration probabilities from 1987 to 2000. However, we cannot distinguish people's immigration status or migration experience as we did with the MMP sample.

The data indicate that 655,000 people crossed from Mexico to the United States in the 12 months prior to the 2000 Mexican Census (Figure 2.3). This is slightly less than the 682,000 who moved to the United States in the 12 months prior to the 1997 ENADID. But both are above the 621,000 who moved 12 months prior to the 1992 ENADID. There has been a decline in the proportion of Mexicans who moved to the United States, as shown by the curves in Figure 2.3. A total of 1.13 percent of the Mexican population moved to the United States in the 12 months prior to the 1992 ENADID; this figure increased to 1.17 percent by the 1997 ENADID and then declined to 1.11 percent by the 2000 Census. This pattern corresponds to that in Figure 2.1, which shows a decline in migration probabilities in the early 1990s, an increase during the economic crisis of the mid 1990s, and a decline in the latter part of the 1990s. This pattern may be an indication of the effectiveness of the border enforcement build-up; however, it may

---

[20]A household informant was asked to identify the usual residents of the household. Then the informant was asked about the migration history of all household members for the past five years, whether they were currently living in the household or not. For more information on the sample, see Appendix A.

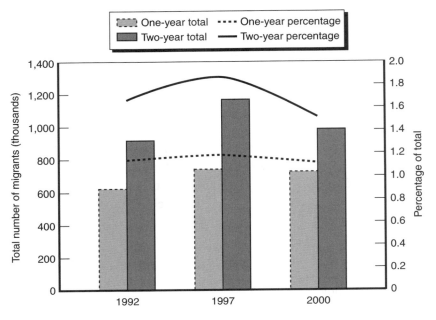

One-year total ···· One-year percentage
Two-year total — Two-year percentage

SOURCES: Mexican 2000 Census and 1992 and 1997 ENADID.

Figure 2.3—Mexicans 15 Years of Age and Older Migrating to the United States Within One and Two Years of the Survey Date

also have been due to changes in the conditions of the U.S. and Mexican economies, as shown in Tables 2.1 and 2.2.

## Immigrants' Accounts of Their Experiences

In the summer of 2000, we conducted five focus groups with unauthorized immigrants in the United States, and in January 2001, we conducted a community survey in one of Mexico's major sending regions of immigrants to the United States.[21] Our purpose was to gather firsthand information on immigrants' impressions about the build-up and how it affects their behavior. The sample is not representative of the whole Mexican immigrant population, so the results cannot be generalized to that population. Rather, the focus groups provide limited

[21]For a description of the data, see Appendix A.

anecdotal accounts of people's experiences, which may help us to understand the circumstances confronting this particular population. Although the accounts cannot be generalized, they are consistent with our statistical analyses and bring a human dimension to the quantitative data.

Almost all the people we spoke with were aware of the recent build-up at the U.S-Mexican border and recognized the increased difficulty in crossing. Almost all of them knew of someone who had been arrested, mistreated, robbed, or killed, and many had their own personal experiences to relate. However, most of the people we talked with stated that the build-up did not deter them from crossing. People described a persistent need to migrate, which they felt could not be diminished by an increase in the number of agents at the border. The following statement summarizes the general consensus of the people we spoke with:

> It does not matter if they keep increasing the patrols. In one whole day of work here, you make 100 pesos. That is about $8, and this is how much you can make in the U.S. per hour. This is why people go north. (Mexico)

Respondents to our survey in Mexico and participants in our focus groups in the United States told us that people move to provide their families with a decent standard of living:

> Today people leave because there is no work here, and since they have to take care of their families, they risk their lives to get there. Many young people cross to go to work in order to help their parents. . . . My sons [four out of five] left because I could not pay for their studies, and they wanted to do something with their lives. (Mexico)

> People have to think about their families, the wife and the children. If they stay in Mexico, nothing is going to change. Their children won't be able to progress. At most, they'll get to primary school or secondary school and that is it. . . . They would not be able to do more. So, they come because of the economy, because of survival. Do you understand? Not for individual reasons, but for family reasons. (Los Angeles)

Respondents on both sides of the border said there were few opportunities in Mexico for their children. Poor children could not afford to go to school, and often they needed to drop out of school to help their families survive:

> My children could not finish high school without Miguel's help [a son living in the United States], because we did not have a cent to buy their

notebooks. My husband used to ask them why they bothered to study if they would not get to graduate. How can a poor family's boy study? Even if my children would have studied, who was going to give them a chance? (Mexico)

Here many children do not finish elementary school, and I think the main reason is because they lack the economic resources. Sometimes they do not even have enough to eat and much less to get school materials. To our store come children that do not even have money to buy a pencil. You can see they need it, but they just do not have enough to buy it. (Mexico)

In our interviews, people spoke about worsening conditions for farmers in Mexico, especially after agricultural reform. Respondents discussed how increasing production costs and declines in the prices of the products they sell in the market have made difficult times even harder. In Mexico, we heard the following explanations:

I buy a 20-kilo sack of "nilo" at 600 pesos, and then after harvest you can sell the ton of product at 1,030 pesos. Can you imagine what happens if you are not able to sell? You also have to pay workers for planting and fertilizing. With that price you cannot make it. People leave because the price is no good and there are no incentives to farm. Even if farmers here were very determined, it is not convenient for them to farm any longer. They prefer to go north and harvest the product for other farmers there. (Mexico)

I believe the government could help by stabilizing the price of seeds and fertilizers and by fixing a fair price for corn. In this way, peasants would be encouraged to work the land and would not go to the U.S. I planted garbanzo beans with an investment of 14,000 pesos, and they wanted to give me 7,000 pesos for the whole lot. Instead of making a living, I was crawling. Now you see how much incentive I have to plant anything again. . . . I better just go north! (Mexico)

Those interviewed also mentioned unmet infrastructure needs. In the town we visited in Mexico, there was no irrigation system for the fields, and people relied on water from wells. In the poorest parts of the town, there had been no water for an entire month:

Young people do not progress because there is not even a high school in town. You need a lot of money to go to Jiquilpan or Zamora. That is why, for example, my son became depressed and decided to go north. (Mexico)

For example, there are villages in my region where for 15 years they've had a plan to put in a road to the village, but they never did it. And it was the people . . . the people who come here . . . they cooperated and put in 50 or 100 dollars each, and they built the road, and that's how my village got a road. And once they saw that the road had been built, then the government sent a machine to widen the road, but they wouldn't do much else to help us. (Madera)

In contrast to the poor economic conditions in Mexico, the opportunities in the United States are far superior for many Mexicans. Wage differences are dramatic, as is the availability of employment:

There's more work, you look and you find work, even if it's seasonal, you go on. When the grapes end, the olives begin. Like now, when the strawberries end, you go to Oregon; when things finish in Oregon, you come here; when the grapes end here, the onions begin; and so one goes, knowing, one follows the seasons. (Madera)

I tell you something, with what you make here in a day, you can eat the entire week. There, they pay you 70 pesos a day, on a good day. Seventy pesos are about $7. A kilogram of meat, which is equivalent to two pounds, costs 47 pesos; so if you buy a kilo of meat and tortillas, with what are you going to buy a pair of pants? Here if you make $50 in a day, you can buy five pounds of meat for about $10. You can still go to a second-hand store and buy a pair of pants for two quarters. (Fresno)

Some of the people we interviewed had to try several times before finally making it across the border. Even so, they did not give up:

A year ago, my son Jorge left to try to go to the U.S. and failed in the attempt. He told me that when the migra was chasing them, the coyote [smuggler] accelerated the van, and since they were driving on a dirt road, the van fell on its side. My son came back very hurt and bleeding. He left all his papers in the van they had abandoned. He does not know if the coyote escaped and returned through the hills, but since nobody came to their assistance, they had to come out however they could. It took four months of doctor visits for him to recover, and as soon as he did, he left again. (Mexico)

I have been lucky, but my son spent three days in the desert. When his legs started hurting, the group he was traveling with left him in the desert. After three more days, he turned himself in to the Border Patrol. He was deported to Mexicali, and from there he called us to ask for money to come home. Still, two months later he returned to the border, paid $1,500 to a coyote, and was able to cross. (Mexico)

Many respondents suggested that people did not give up because they borrowed money to make the trip, and if they returned they would have to pay the money back. In Madera, a migrant explained:

But look, what happens is that there are many people that when they are going to come here, they borrow money at 10 or 15 percent interest so they can come here. Now, if they make the effort and arrive at the border and they can't get across, and they try again and the INS grabs them, they have to continue struggling, because they are spending the money—for food, for lunch, and to pay the coyote. So they have to keep trying to get across, because they can't go back. . . . They have to make an effort to come here in order to be able to pay the money. Because if they don't, they'll take your house, they'll take everything, and instead of earning something by coming north, you'll have to sell your house, sell your land, to pay the debt. (Madera)

Many respondents believe that despite the dangers of the trip, most people cross successfully. For instance, we heard from a woman in Mexico:

People today take more risks in order to survive and get ahead in life. It was hard to cross before, and now, even though it is harder, most of those attempting the crossing are able to make it. (Mexico)

Another migrant explained:

Well, they come following others, and of 20 or 30 who come, they simply catch . . . two, three . . . but even they get across, they cross. . . . It costs them, but they get across. (Los Angeles)

Almost all of the people in our sample were aware of the risks of crossing. A few months before our visit to Mexico, a couple from the community we surveyed had died in the desert, and many respondents spoke to us about it. However, they either rationalized the deaths as the result of some mistake or they thought it was a matter of luck or fate:

Recently they brought in two bodies of two young kids that died at the border. Their bodies were decomposing and animals ate them up. But people continue the same. They take it as if it was negligence: "If they would have done this, if they would have done that . . . they were incommunicado, maybe they were detained." (Mexico)

A man in Mexico explained:

Entering the north is a thing of luck. A guy that was trying to cross for 21 days came back yesterday, and another left and crossed the same day. It is a thing of luck. (Mexico)

Other people, especially the few people we talked to from Central America or from new sending regions in Mexico, told us that many migrants do not talk about their bad migration experiences. Thus, others at home may not be fully aware of the risks. These respondents argued that people talk only about the wages they are making in the United States and not about how hard life is for them or how hard it is to cross. We also noticed that women were more willing to talk about their bad experiences than men, especially if there were other men in the room when we were conducting the interview. A woman in Los Angeles told us:

> I have a brother who wants to come. I said, "There are many people who come and go and come back." I said, "They only talk about dollars, why don't they talk about getting hurt on the hill when they ran?" Most people have to tell that story, not only the good side. I was never told you had to run, you had to do this; it always was, "Oh, you're going to make good money." Nobody talks about the crossing, nobody. The people I heard from always talked about the money, Disneyland . . . ooh, wonderful things. Out of 10, maybe one tells the truth. (Los Angeles)

## Summary

For first-time migrants, the probability of moving to the United States as an unauthorized immigrant increased through most of the 1980s. It declined for the first time in 10 years during the economic downturn of the early 1990s in the United States and then increased again during the economic crisis of the mid 1990s in Mexico that led to the devaluation of the peso. Another decline in the probability of first migration occurred during the enforcement period in the latter part of the 1990s.

Our models indicate that the border build-up has not had an independent effect on the probability of migration for either first-time or experienced migrants. Although we observe a decline in the probability of migration for first-time migrants during the period of enforcement, there is no statistically significant effect of the build-up, as measured by the total number of line watch hours, on the probability of migration.

We do find, however, that economic opportunities in the U.S. and Mexican economies play an important role in determining migration probabilities. As the U.S. economy deteriorates, migration from Mexico declines. As the Mexican economy grows, outmigration declines. Like other researchers, we also found a dramatic increase in the probability of migration in the few years following the passage of IRCA (Johnson, 1996; Warren, 2000).

# 3. Has Increased Border Enforcement Altered the Duration of Stay in the United States?

An increase in border enforcement could lead to a change in the length of time immigrants stay in the United States, perhaps by changing what would have been a cyclical or temporary migration into a longer-term or permanent migration. Having to face higher risks and greater crossing costs, migrants could increase the duration of their stay, and these longer stays could increase the total number of immigrants living in the United States at any one time.

In this chapter, we examine unauthorized immigrants' length of stay in the United States[1] in order to determine the effect of the build-up on the probability of return independent of other factors such as changes in immigrants' characteristics or in economic conditions. We use the MMP to model the length of immigrant stays in the United States from 1970 until 1998.[2] We also use three nationally representative samples from

---

[1]The model looks at the probability of return, holding constant the length of stay in the United States. That is, the models estimate the time that elapses before return. Throughout this chapter, we discuss the probability of returning by a certain time period—for example, within the first year of migration. We take this measure to be synonymous with duration of stay.

[2]We selected a sample of people who moved without documents to the United States to determine how long they stayed there. However, many people readjusted their status after IRCA, and others readjusted their status through the 245i program. (Section 245i of the Immigration and Nationality Act, an amendment enacted in 1990, permits foreigners in the United States eligible to become legal immigrants to adjust their status in the United States rather than return to their home countries and obtain an immigrant visa from the U.S. consulate.) We do not take this into account in the models presented in this chapter. Instead, we look at the possibility of legalization by including a dummy variable for having another family member who has been legalized. However, this may

Mexico—the 1992 and 1997 ENADID and the Mexican 2000 Census—for further evidence.[3] We use these data to model the probability of return for those who moved to the United States two years prior to the survey year.[4]

We find that the probability of return within the first year of migration increased in the latter part of the 1980s and the early 1990s, then declined in the 1990s, especially during the period of increased enforcement. As a result, even if the number of new immigrants declines, a greater number of immigrants may live in the United States because those who cross stay longer.

## Duration of Stay in the United States: Traditional Sending Communities, 1970–1998

Figure 3.1 shows the proportion of unauthorized immigrants in the MMP sample that returned to Mexico within the first year of migration, controlling for other factors.[5] For men, the probability of return within a year of migration was close to 11 percent before the passage of IRCA. Soon after IRCA, however, the probability of return increased to over 16 percent.[6] In the previous chapter, we found that more people were moving illegally after the passage of IRCA, but it appears that many of

---

not fully capture people's opportunities for legalization and its effect on return probabilities. In another model, we included a dummy variable for changing status; the inclusion of this variable does not change the trend described in this chapter.

[3]For details on the data sources, see Appendix A.

[4]We look at only two years prior to the survey year because there is a possibility of censoring in the Mexican data; longer-term migrants may no longer be considered household members and may therefore be excluded from the sample.

[5]We hold constant for age, education, headship status, the migration experience of other household members (as measured by having a family member who has been in the United States in the last 10 years), and whether someone in the household has been legalized. We try to account for the family's resources by controlling for whether or not the family owns its home or land. We also hold constant for community characteristics (whether the community is small, medium, or large; the proportion of men employed in agriculture; and a dummy for Mexican state). We account for the migrants' experience in the United States by holding constant the number of trips, occupation while in the United States, and place of destination. A full description of the model is presented in Appendix B.

[6]Similar findings were found by Durand, Massey, and Zenteno (2000) for the period after IRCA.

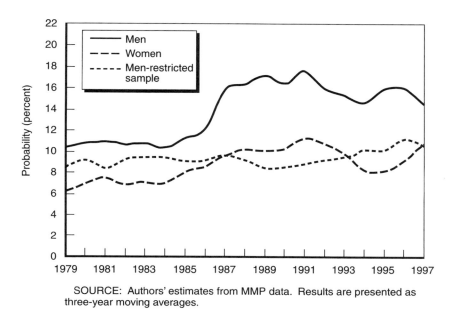

SOURCE: Authors' estimates from MMP data. Results are presented as three-year moving averages.

**Figure 3.1—Probability of Returning to Mexico Within One Year After Migrating to the United States**

them were only making short trips to the United States.[7]  Some unauthorized immigrants could have come to the United States to visit their newly legalized family members, while others may have made temporary trips to try to legalize their status.  Also, many of the people granted legal permanent status could now be moving freely across the U.S.-Mexican border (Durand, Massey, and Zenteno, 2000).  Starting in 1992, the probability of return within a year of migration declined. Although still above pre-IRCA levels, that probability was lower during the build-up period than it was in the late 1980s.  A smaller proportion of women than men return within the first year after migration, but there have been changes over time.  In 1981, the probability of return within one year of migration was only about 7 percent.  By the early 1990s, the probability of return had grown to over 10 percent.  Between 1993 and

---

[7]For the most part, the year-to-year differences in the proportion of people who return are statistically different from one another at a 5 percent level.

1996, the probability of return declined for women, but it later increased in 1997 and 1998.

Figure 3.1 also shows that most of the IRCA effect was concentrated among the major sending regions. When we restrict the sample to communities surveyed after 1994, which are primarily new sending regions, return probabilities are relatively flat.[8] This could be because most of the people legalized through IRCA were from the western part of Mexico; hence, the policy affected the return rates of people in those regions only.

Although these percentage changes are small, the total effect on the unauthorized immigrant population in the United States is quite large. We measure the effect of fewer men returning by looking at a simulation of the cumulative probability of return for men who entered the United States in 1985, 1988, 1991, and 1994 (see Figure 3.2). In 1988, 69 percent of those who entered the United States returned within the

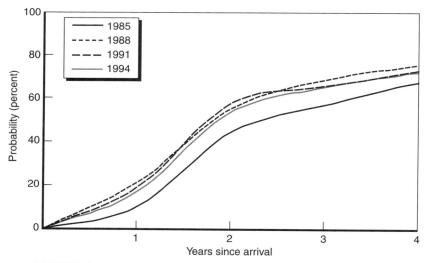

SOURCE: Authors' estimates from MMP data.

**Figure 3.2—Percent of Unauthorized Immigrants Who Return to Mexico Within Four Years After Migration**

---

[8]Sample size limitations prevented us from looking at return rates for women migrants in the restricted sample.

first three years after migration, compared with 65 percent of those who moved in 1994. Assuming that 600,000 men entered illegally in both years, 24,000 more men would still be in the United States after three years if they moved in 1994 than if they moved in 1988, for reasons other than those captured in the model.

What led to this change? As we did for the probability of migration in the previous chapter, we use a set of models to explore the effect of economic conditions in Mexico and the United States, as well as changes in U.S. immigration policy, on the probability of return.[9] These models are presented in Table 3.1.[10]

Of all the macro factors, IRCA appears to have the strongest effect on the probability of return of Mexican immigrants. In 1989, 1,090,900 immigrants were either admitted as legal immigrants or granted legal permanent status; this is 660,000 more than in 1988. This pattern increased the probability of return within the first year of migration by 4 percent. Assuming 600,000 immigrants enter per year, the IRCA effect would result in 24,000 more men returning within the first year of migration. Some researchers argue that many more people than expected entered the country in the IRCA period seeking legalization, especially under the Special Agricultural Workers provision of IRCA (Martin, 1994). It is also possible that many people entered the United States temporarily to join family members who had been legalized.

In most of our models, the build-up at the U.S.-Mexican border has a negative effect on the probability of return, which indicates that as more resources and agents are allocated to the border, unauthorized migrants tend to stay longer in the United States. This effect, however, is statistically significant only in the model without controls, indicating that either the effect was too small as of 1998 to be captured by these

---

[9]For details on the modeling in this chapter, see Appendix B.

[10]The first model examines the effect of conditions in Mexico and the United States without controlling for changes in the sample. The second model examines the effect of conditions in the United States and Mexico on the probability of return after controlling for changes in the household, community, and personal characteristics. The last model shows the effect of economic conditions and immigration policy on the restricted sample of communities surveyed after 1994, in which new sending regions are oversampled.

## Table 3.1

### Parameter Estimates and Standard Errors for the Second-Stage OLS Equation: Model of the Probability of Return (MMP)[11]

|  | Men | | | Women | | |
|---|---|---|---|---|---|---|
|  | No Controls | With Controls | Restricted Sample | No Controls | With Controls | Restricted Sample |
| Intercept | −0.53 | −1.01** | −0.56 | −0.32 | −1.39* | −0.48 |
|  | (0.48) | (0.49) | (0.56) | (0.63) | (0.71) | (1.2) |
| Conditions of the Mexican economy | | | | | | |
| Mexican GDP per | 0.0003 | 0.0003 | 0.00002 | 0.0005 | 0.0003 | −0.0008 |
| capita | (0.0003) | (0.0003) | (0.0004) | (0.0004) | (0.0004) | (0.0007) |
| Mexican GDP squared | −0.0007 | −0.0005 | −0.0001 | −0.0009 | −0.0006 | 0.001 |
|  | (0.0005) | (0.0005) | (0.0005) | (0.0006) | (0.0007) | (0.001) |
| Exchange rate | 0.03 | 0.06 | −0.03 | −0.08 | −0.04 | −0.08 |
|  | (0.06) | (0.06) | (0.06) | (0.07) | (0.08) | (0.12) |
| Conditions of the U.S. economy | | | | | | |
| U.S. unemployment | −0.06 | −0.07 | −0.05 | −0.09 | −0.08 | −0.034 |
| rate | (0.05) | (0.05) | (0.06) | (0.06) | (0.07) | (0.12) |
| U.S. immigration policy | | | | | | |
| Legal admissions | 0.225* | 0.29** | 0.13 | 0.44*** | 0.47** | 0.578** |
|  | (0.127) | (0.13) | (0.14) | (0.15) | (0.17) | (0.27) |
| Legal admissions | −0.009 | −0.011* | −0.006 | −0.018** | −0.018** | −0.02** |
| squared | (0.005) | (0.006) | (0.005) | (0.006) | (0.007) | (0.01) |
| Line watch hours | −0.77** | −0.17 | 0.25 | −1.06** | −0.6 | −0.58 |
|  | (0.36) | (0.37) | (0.39) | (0.44) | (0.49) | (0.79) |
| Line watch hours | 0.07 | 0.0009 | −0.019 | 0.14** | 0.085 | 0.1 |
| squared | (0.04) | (0.04) | (0.04) | (0.05) | (0.06) | (0.08) |
| $R^2$ | 53% | 65% | 27% | 47% | 55% | 31% |
| Adjusted R | 34% | 52% | −2% | 26% | 37% | 3% |

NOTES: **** = significant at a 1 percent level; *** = significant at a 5 percent level; ** = significant at a 10 percent level.

---

[11] During this period of the analysis, the average GDP per capita in Mexico was 2,643 pesos, the Mexican economy grew by 4 percent, 700,000 people per year were legally admitted to the United States, the unemployment rate in the United States was 6.7 percent, and the INS spent on average 2.6 million man-hours guarding the U.S.-Mexican border. The GDP is normalized to 100 pesos, the legal admissions to 100,000, and the number of hours to 1 million.

models or that other factors are at play. To get a more recent picture of the changes in duration of stay and to confirm the patterns observed with the MMP data, we look at the Mexican 2000 Census and the 1992 and 1997 ENADID.

## Duration of Stay in the United States: The National Sample, 1987–2000

In this section, we use the Mexican 2000 Census and ENADID data to determine changes in the probability of migration in the 1990s. These data are nationally representative samples of households in Mexico and should therefore not suffer from the sample selection problems that could be present in a preselected sample of communities. Unlike the MMP data, these datasets do not contain information on immigrants' legal status. However, we believe that most of the people in the sample are unauthorized immigrants.[12]

As shown below, a smaller proportion of immigrants returned to Mexico in 1995–2000 than in previous periods (see Figure 3.3). In the post-IRCA period of 1987 to 1992, 54 percent of the immigrants in the sample returned to Mexico by the time of the survey, whereas only 25 percent returned to Mexico between 1995 and 2000, the period of greatest border enforcement. Figure 3.4 shows that the duration of stay in the United States by those who eventually return to Mexico has increased. In the post-IRCA period, those who returned to Mexico had lived on average 10 months in the United States. Those who returned to Mexico during the period of increased border enforcement had lived in the United States for almost 16 months.

It is difficult to determine whether increased enforcement or other factors have led to increases in duration of stay. We use ENADID and Mexican 2000 Census data to model the probability of return for an individual who moved to the United States 24 months prior to the survey date (1992, 1997, or 2000). We consider how the length of stay in the United States has changed over time, holding constant for

---

[12]Only in the 1992 ENADID were immigrants asked about their immigration status while in the United States; 80 percent of the immigrants were unauthorized.

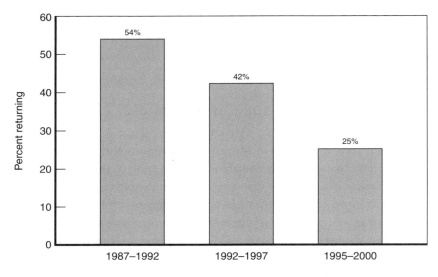

SOURCES: 1992 and 1997 ENADID and Mexican 2000 Census.

NOTE: These proportions have been standardized by years since departure (within the past five years). Nonstandardized patterns are similar, with 46 percent of migrants having returned to Mexico in 1987–1992, 35 percent in 1992–1997, and 23 percent in 1995–2000.

**Figure 3.3—Return Migration Rates**

personal and household characteristics, as well as characteristics of the immigrant's community of origin.[13]

The ENADID data show that of the people who moved to the United States two years earlier, about 20 percent returned to Mexico within the first six months after migration, and of those who moved in 1995, 15 percent returned within six months (Figure 3.5). However, the Mexican 2000 Census shows that only 7 percent of those who moved two years earlier had returned to Mexico after six months. In other words, if 600,000 immigrants enter illegally every year, 120,000 more migrants would have stayed in the United States for longer than a year in the latter part of the 1990s than in the early 1990s. Our analysis of the

---

[13]These characteristics include the immigrant's age and sex, the material of the floors in the home, the number of members in the household, the state of origin, and the size of the community of origin.

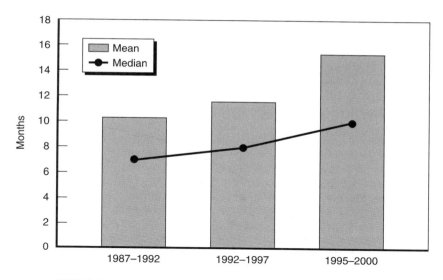

SOURCES: 1992 and 1997 ENADID and Mexican 2000 Census.

Figure 3.4—Average Length of Stay in the United States by Migrants Who
Returned to Mexico: Men and Women over 15 Years of Age

MMP data captures changes in duration of stay through 1998. But, as
Figure 3.5 shows, the probability of return had declined only slightly by
1998.

## Immigrant Responses to Changes in Length of Stay in the United States

Our interviews with migrants provide some anecdotal support for
the quantitative findings presented in this chapter.[14] Respondents
mentioned having to stay longer in the United States after the build-up,
for three basic reasons:

- The increased risk and difficulty of going back and forth
  between Mexico and the United States,
- Higher migration costs, which require a longer stay to repay, and

---

[14]For a description of the qualitative data, see Appendix A.

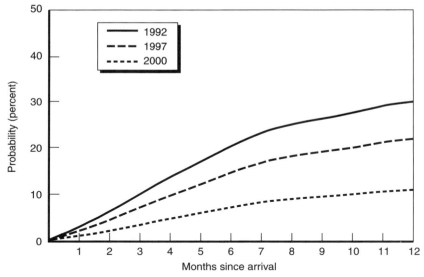

NOTE: Results are presented as three-year moving averages.

**Figure 3.5—Cumulative Probability of Return Based on INEGI Data Generated from the Time-Hazard Model**

- The desire to legalize one's status to make it easier to move back and forth between Mexico and the United States without fear of apprehension.

Many we interviewed said they were afraid that if they returned to Mexico they would not be able to reenter the United States because it is so difficult to cross:

> It has been already four years since my children left because my mom became ill. They went only to save money to pay the doctor bills, but they did not come back . . . because then how would they be able to return to the U.S. afterwards? (Mexico)

Others said they had to stay longer because they had to pay so much more money to cross than they did in the past:

> There are hundreds of people, and thousands of people who work for the minimum, in restaurants, in factories . . . and the minimum is $5.75. . . . Then, with much work and much effort, they put together . . . the money they got from their brothers, their cousins. They pay in installments. And that's how they do it. . . . To pay five thousand something . . . well it will take them

about 2 years. . . . But we all, the majority of us, have family in Mexico . . . and we send money home . . . we also have to pay for an apartment and food here . . . our home. . . . Then you have what, three years; you need three years to pay the money. (Los Angeles)

In Fresno, we heard the following statement:

To be able to pay $1,500 to $2,000 [to a coyote], it takes people at least a year . . . but what happens is that the $1,500 you got cannot be paid as soon as you start working, since you also have to eat . . . and now when you borrow money, you also have to pay interest; every month they charge 10 percent, then it takes longer because of the interest. . . . Because most people come to do seasonal work, for a short time, you know, and in such amount of time, they don't get to even save for the "coyote" . . . [they have] to wait until next season. . . . And they get into more debt. So, even if they didn't like it, they have to stay to pay back the money, and then go back. (Fresno)

An increase in the build-up could also make it more important for people to legalize their immigration status. In our limited sample, some said they are staying longer in the United States with the hope of legalizing their status, enabling them to go back and forth between Mexico and the United States without employment or legal barriers. In Mexico, some explained that their family members were not able to return because they did not have papers and were waiting to legalize their status:

My daughter Maria says that once she has papers, it will be easy for her to come every year to visit, but that now it is too difficult. She says her husband needs two more years to legalize her situation. (Mexico)

The sister of several young men who had just left for the United States explained:

Just now three of my brothers left: Jesus, Jose, and, Fernando, who is only 16 and is on his first trip. They hired a coyote and will pay $1,200 each. They will go through the hills and we are very worried. We have been crying all day, but I tell my mom that rather than crying we should be praying. Jesus had not been back in three years precisely because he feared the crossing. He says that they have to walk and run a lot and pay the coyote so much sometimes just to be deported later. They begin working and paying for the coyote, but there is not always work in the fields. They say that if they had papers, they would come see my mom every year and would live without worries. Jose has not been back in four years for the same reasons as Jesus. (Mexico)

But after having spent many years in the United States, some people change their expectations about return (Massey et al., 1987). Many become accustomed to life in the United States and readjust their plans. Some begin to bring their family members to the United States to resettle completely:

> To tell you truth, it's not that I want to stay, but once you are here, you get used to it. The comfort you have here, you can't get there. Even with things being more expensive here, you make money a little easier than in Mexico. It's hard to make money in Mexico . . . it's easier to have a car or air conditioner here. All the comforts are better here than there. I want to go back, but I wouldn't get used to it again. (Fresno)

> Well, I went back in '95, you know, and I wanted to work during the four months I was going to be there. But I realized that what they pay there, it wasn't enough, you know. I couldn't get used to being there. And it's true, in this country you have more comfort, so it seems you learn something: to live in a different way. So it's hard for you to adapt back to what you came from. And that's why you don't force yourself to live there again. (Fresno)

## Summary

The findings based on both the national data and the MMP sample indicate a decline in the probability of return in the 1990s. Analysis of the MMP sample shows no statistically significant effect of the build-up on the probability of return. But the INEGI data indicate a continuing decline in the probability of return in the latter part of the 1990s, which could be the result of an increase in border enforcement. This possibility is also suggested by our interviews in both Mexico and the United States.

In the previous chapter, we found no significant effect of the build-up on the probability of first migration, which declined in the late 1990s. We also found no effect of the build-up on the probability of migration among experienced migrants. However, our analysis of the restricted sample indicates that the build-up may have increased the probability of migration in new sending regions.[15] In this chapter, we find a dramatic decline in the probability of return in the late 1990s. The combined

---

[15]This finding could also be a reflection of the way communities were selected into the MMP sample. It is possible that these regions were chosen in the MMP because they experienced increases in migration during the 1990s for reasons other than the build-up.

effect of these three migration patterns could be an increase in the number of unauthorized immigrants living in the United States in the mid to late 1990s. This will be explored in the next chapter.

# 4. Has Increased Border Enforcement Decreased Unauthorized Immigration?

In this chapter, we consider the effect of increased border enforcement on the number of unauthorized immigrants residing in the United States and on the annual flow of unauthorized immigrants. In Chapter 2 and Chapter 3, we found some evidence of a decline in the probability of illegal immigration in the late 1990s, but the evidence also indicated that the duration of stay of those who crossed had increased.[1] Lower probabilities of migrating lead to lower numbers of people entering the United States illegally, but longer lengths of stay lead to a greater number of unauthorized immigrants in the United States.

Estimating both the number of unauthorized immigrants residing in the United States and the flow of unauthorized residents is a complex undertaking. Unauthorized immigrants often seek to avoid detection, and legal status is not recorded in any nationally representative survey of the U.S. population. In our analyses, we use data from both the United States and Mexico. The primary U.S. datasets we and other researchers rely on to examine trends in unauthorized migration flows and populations are the Current Population Survey (CPS) and the decennial censuses. The primary Mexican datasets include surveys conducted by INEGI and the Mexican 2000 Census. These datasets complement one another and enable a more comprehensive analysis than can be performed by looking at data from only one side of the border. In particular, the CPS is likely to capture more long-term and permanent settlers in the United States, whereas the Mexican data are likely to

---

[1]Importantly, we did not find that increased enforcement explained the decline in the probability of migrating to the United States. That is, much of the change seems to be due to other factors.

capture more temporary and cyclical migrants (see Appendix A for a discussion of the data sources). We present the work of other researchers as well as our own estimates to determine changes in the number and flow of unauthorized immigrants as border enforcement has increased. In addition, we consider whether particular labor markets exhibit shortages of low-skill workers, since unauthorized immigrants tend to be concentrated in certain low-skill occupations.

We find that the number of unauthorized immigrants residing in the United States is at an all-time high. Moreover, increases in the unauthorized population residing in the United States appear to have been very large in the 1990s. Estimates of the annual flow of unauthorized immigrants are uncertain, but they seem to indicate that flows into the United States were very high during the period just after IRCA (the late 1980s and 1990), then they declined with the recession of the early 1990s and increased substantially in the very late 1990s. The events that temporally correspond with these patterns are IRCA and economic cycles in the United States rather than increased border enforcement. As formerly unauthorized immigrants were granted legalization in the late 1980s under IRCA, they sent for family members and friends to join them in the United States, many of whom were unauthorized (Johnson, 1996; Calavita, 1994). Many others could have entered the United States temporarily in an attempt to legalize their status under IRCA, especially under the Special Agricultural Workers provision. The apparent slowdown in the flows of the early 1990s and the increases in the late 1990s correspond with the recession and recovery in the United States. The period of greatest border enforcement, the late 1990s, appears to coincide with a large increase in the number of unauthorized immigrants in the United States. Almost certainly, the number of unauthorized farm workers increased substantially as border enforcement levels increased.

In this chapter, we first summarize the methods used to estimate unauthorized immigration. We then present estimates of the number of unauthorized immigrants living in the United States. Next, we discuss estimates of the flow of unauthorized immigrants based on U.S. data.

We then consider estimates of the flow of immigrants from Mexico using Mexican data sources. Finally, we consider evidence of labor shortages among farm workers in the United States.

## Methods Used to Estimate Unauthorized Immigration

Numerous methods have been employed to estimate unauthorized immigration. These estimates can be classified as either *stock* estimates or *flow* estimates. Stock estimates of unauthorized immigrants are population estimates for a given date, whereas flow estimates attempt to measure changes over some period of time. Most estimates of unauthorized immigrants are stock estimates, although estimates of the flow have become more important and common.

Methods used to develop estimates of the number of unauthorized immigrants range from speculative guesses to analytic techniques using large datasets.[2] The estimates presented below are analytic, and almost all rely on a technique known as the residual method. In this method, the unauthorized immigrant population is determined by subtracting an estimate of foreign-born legal residents of the United States from an estimate of all foreign-born persons in the United States. Adjustments are sometimes made for misreporting of place of birth and undercoverage of immigrant populations. Further adjustments are sometimes made for persons of ambiguous legal status (see, for example, Bean et al., 2001). Estimates of the annual flow or annual change in the unauthorized immigrant population are generally determined by taking the difference between stock estimates at different points in time.

Increasingly, demographers develop several estimates for the same time point by altering underlying assumptions. The resultant range of estimates can be quite wide, but it accurately conveys the uncertainty of the size of the unauthorized immigrant population in the United States.

---

[2]See PPIC Working Paper, "Methods Used to Estimate Unauthorized Immigration," for a more complete discussion.

# Unauthorized Immigrants Living in the United States: Estimates of the Stock

Estimates of the number of unauthorized immigrants in the United States developed before the release of the 2000 Census counts tend to be much lower than those developed after the 2000 Census numbers were released. One of the surprises of the 2000 Census was that it counted more residents of the United States than previous estimates had suggested. The difference between the Census Bureau's own pre-Census estimate of the nation's population on April 1, 2000, and the Census count totaled 6.8 million people (without adjustments for the undercount),[3] much of this being due to greater growth of Hispanic and foreign-born populations than had been estimated. After adjustment for the undercount, estimates of the nation's population showed an even greater difference (10.1 million). There are at least five possible reasons for the higher U.S. population in 2000 than was predicted by earlier estimates:

- The 1990 Census had a much greater undercount than was previously believed,
- Emigration from the United States during the 1990s was much lower than had been estimated,
- Legal immigration, particularly flows of nonimmigrants,[4] was higher than had been estimated,
- The 2000 Census counted more temporary and cyclical migrants than the 1990 Census did, and
- Unauthorized migration to the United States was substantially higher than previously estimated.

The large difference between the estimates and the 2000 Census results is probably attributable to a combination of the reasons listed above, and it is likely that high levels of unauthorized migration contributed to the discrepancy. Researchers at the Census Bureau, the

---

[3]The net undercount is the number of people missed by the Census minus those counted twice.

[4]Nonimmigrants are international migrants to the United States who are not legal permanent residents—for example, people with temporary work and student visas.

Urban Institute, and the INS, among others, are revising estimates of unauthorized immigration, using 2000 Census results.

Table 4.1 shows estimates of unauthorized populations in the United States developed by several researchers. These estimates vary according to the methodology employed and the data source used, but they suggest a large and growing population of unauthorized immigrants. For example, preliminary estimates of the 2000 population of unauthorized immigrants developed by the Census Bureau place the total at somewhere between 7.7 million and 8.8 million (Deardorff and Blumerman, 2001). The most recent estimates for 2001 place the total

**Table 4.1**

**Estimates of Unauthorized Immigrants in the United States, 1980–2000**

| Source | Date of Estimate | Number of Unauthorized Immigrants |
|---|---|---|
| Bean, King, and Passel (1983a) | 1980 | 1.5 million to 3.9 million (Mexicans) |
| Warren and Passel (1987) | 1980 | 2.1 million in the Census 2.5 million to 3.5 million total |
| Passel and Woodrow (1987) | 1980 | 1.7 million (aged 14 and over ) in the Census |
| Passel and Woodrow (1987) | 1983 | 2.1 million (aged 14 and over) in the CPS |
| Woodrow, Passel, and Warren (1987) | June 1986 | 3.2 million (range of 3.0 million to 5.0 million) |
| Woodrow and Passel (1990) | June 1988 | 1.6 million (range of 1.1 million to 1.9 million) |
| Warren (1994) | October 1988 | 0.9 million |
| Clark, Passel, Zimmerman, and Fix (1994) | 1990 | 2.0 million in the 1990 Census |
| Woodrow (1991) | April 1990 | 2.1 million in the Census (range of 1.6 million to 2.7 million), 3.3 million total (range of 1.9 million to 4.5 million) |
| Woodrow-Lafield, in Bean et al. (1998) | April 1990 | 2.3 million in the Census, 2.3 million to 5.0 million total |
| Robinson (1994) | April 1990 | 2.2 million in the Census, 3.3 million total |

Table 4.1 (continued)

| Source | Date of Estimate | Number of Unauthorized Immigrants |
|---|---|---|
| Robinson (1994) | October 1992 | 3.8 million total |
| Warren (1994) | 1992 | 3.4 million |
| Fernandez and Robinson (1994) | 1992 | 3.5 million to 4.0 million |
| Warren (1997) | 1996 | 5.0 million |
| Passel (2001a) | March 1995 | 5.0 million in the CPS |
| Passel and Fix (2001) | March 2000 | 7.0 million in the CPS |
| Passel and Fix (2001) | April 2000 | 8.5 million in the Census, 9.0 million in the ACE[a] (Census adjusted for undercount) |
| Warren (2000)[b] | January 1987 | 1.06 million Mexicans, 2.08 million total |
| Warren (2000)[b] | January 1990 | 1.85 million Mexicans, 3.48 million total |
| Warren (2000)[b] | January 1995 | 2.84 million Mexicans, 4.92 million total |
| Warren (2000)[b] | January 1997 | 3.07 million Mexicans, 5.12 million total |
| Bean et al. (2001) | March 1996 | 2.54 million Mexicans |
| Bean et al. (2001) | April 2000 | 3.9 million Mexicans, 7.1 million total |
| Costanzo et al. (2002) | April 1990 | 3.8 million unauthorized and quasi-legal immigrants counted in the Census, 4.4 million total |
| Costanzo et al. (2002) | April 2000 | 8.7 million unauthorized and quasi-legal immigrants counted in the Census, 10.2 million total |
| Deardorff and Blumerman (2001) | April 2000 | 7.7 million to 8.8 million total |
| Bean, Van Hook, and Woodrow-Lafield (2001) | 2001 | 7.8 million total, range of 5.9 million to 9.9 million; 4.5 million Mexicans (range of 3.4 million to 5.8 million) |

[a]Accurary and Coverage Evaluation.

[b]These estimates contain "known data deficiencies," according to the author (personal communication). We provide them for comparison purposes and note that they were made publicly available and widely disseminated by Representative Lamar Smith, Chair of the Subcommittee on Immigration and Claims, Committee on the Judiciary, U.S. House of Representatives. The 1987 estimate does not include immigrants who were later legalized under IRCA.

at somewhere between 5.9 million and 9.9 million (Bean, Van Hook, and Woodrow-Lafield, 2001). These estimates represent a large increase over the population in the mid 1990s—both Warren (2000) and Passel (2001a) place the population of unauthorized immigrants at around 5 million in 1996. As shown in Figure 4.1, the number of unauthorized immigrants in the United States has grown tremendously over time, with the only notable decline occurring as a result of IRCA, which allowed millions of unauthorized migrants to become legal permanent residents in the late 1980s.

However, as discussed earlier, some of the apparent increases during the 1990s might not be real; that is, they may reflect coverage differences between the data sources and even within a particular data source over time. In particular, the 2000 Census may have missed far fewer unauthorized immigrants than the 1990 Census did. Outreach efforts to encourage participation in the 2000 Census were far more extensive than

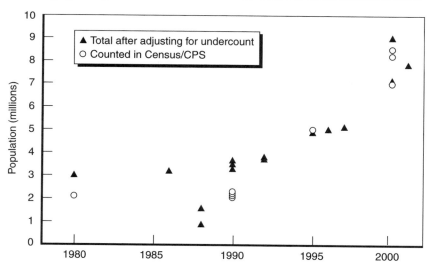

NOTES: Each point represents an estimate from a particular source, as shown in Table 4.1. For some years, more than one estimate has been developed. In these cases, we take the midpoint of high and low estimates.

Figure 4.1—Estimates of the Number of Unauthorized Immigrants in the United States, 1980–2001

those for previous censuses, and greater participation may have even spilled over to the March 2000 CPS. If so, the apparent large increases in the population of unauthorized immigrants between the mid 1990s and 2000 result at least partly from better coverage. For example, if the undercount rate dropped dramatically, from 33 percent in 1995 to only 7 percent in 2000 (as suggested by Passel's analysis for 2000), the growth of the unauthorized population of the United States was much less dramatic. Applying a 33 percent undercount in 1995 to Passel's estimates from the CPS gives a total unauthorized immigrant population in the United States of about 7.1 million rather than 5.0 million.[5] These very rough adjustments suggest that rather than growing by over 3 million during the last part of the 1990s, the unauthorized population might have grown by less than 2 million.

Nonetheless, by the turn of the century, the number of unauthorized immigrants in the United States was at its highest level ever, much higher even than the level prior to the legalization program of the late 1980s. Moreover, estimates based on the March 2001 CPS suggest that the number of unauthorized immigrants in the United States is around 7.8 million. This is noteworthy because the March 2001 CPS was not likely to be greatly affected by Census outreach. Regardless of which estimates are used, the number of unauthorized immigrants in the United States increased dramatically during the 1990s.

## Unauthorized Immigration Flows: Estimates from U.S. Data

Estimates of the flow of unauthorized immigrants are even more uncertain than stock estimates. No point-in-time estimate shown in Table 4.1 is precise, even if we ignore undercount issues. For example, Warren places a range of plus or minus 400,000 around his estimate of 5 million unauthorized immigrants in 1996. Subtracting uncertain point-in-time estimates for different dates leads to even more uncertain estimates of the net increase in the unauthorized population. Also, it is important to distinguish between temporal increases in the number of

---

[5]Fernandez and Robinson used a 33 percent undercount rate in their 1990 Census estimates (Fernandez and Robinson, 1994).

unauthorized immigrants residing in the United States (changes in the stock) and the net flow of unauthorized immigrants to the United States. The change in the number of unauthorized immigrants residing in the United States from one date to the next does not equal net unauthorized immigration between those dates. Declines in the stock of unauthorized immigrants in the United States occur as those residents emigrate, adjust to a legal status, or die. Increases occur through unauthorized immigration and as some people (primarily temporary visa holders) lose their legal status. Thus, net annual changes in the population of unauthorized immigrants can serve only as a rough estimate for net flows across the border. Finally, as noted above, coverage improvements in the 2000 Census and the CPS could lead to an overstatement of recent increases in the unauthorized population.

Differences in stock estimates for different years prior to the 1990s suggest that net annual additions to the unauthorized immigrant population were between 100,000 and 300,000. The U.S. Census Bureau used these differenced results to estimate and project the population of the United States, stating:

> There are no regular administrative data sources for determining a precise number of undocumented residents in the United States. However, several coordinated research activities lead us to believe that this population is increasing by approximately 200,000 per year. (Word, 1992)

Since then, estimates of the net annual increase in unauthorized immigrants to the United States have risen. During the 1990s, the Census Bureau estimated net annual increases of 281,000 for 1990 through 1992 and 275,000 for the rest of the decade (Passel, 2001b). However, in light of the 2000 Census, even these higher estimates now seem too low.

Table 4.2 shows average annual changes in the population of unauthorized immigrants in the United States.[6] These figures include the period of the most recent increase in border enforcement, but they are estimates, not a direct measure of unauthorized immigration flows.

---

[6]Net annual changes in the population of unauthorized immigrants is equal to unauthorized inmigration less unauthorized outmigration less adjustments to legal status less deaths plus those who lose their legal status.

## Table 4.2

### Estimates of Average Annual Growth in the Population of Unauthorized Immigrants in the United States, 1980–2000

| Source | Time Period | Average Annual Population Growth |
|---|---|---|
| Passel and Woodrow (1987) | 1980-1983 | 100,000 to 300,000 (aged 14+ only) |
| Woodrow, Passel, and Warren (1987) | 1980-1986 | 176,000 |
| Warren (1990) | 1985-1988 | 217,000 to 255,000 |
| Warren (2000) | 1988-1992 | 436,000[a] |
|  | 1992-1996 | 146,000 |
| Passel and Fix (2001) | Early 1990s | 275,000 |
|  | Late 1990s | 400,000 to 500,000 |
| Bean et al. (2001) | 1996-2000 | 625,000[b] |

[a]Does not include the decrement due to IRCA legalizations.

[b]We calculated this estimate based the estimate of Bean et al. of the Mexican unauthorized population and their estimate that Mexicans constitute 55 percent of the unauthorized population of the United States. Sample and coverage differences between the 1996 and 2000 estimates are thus incorporated in this estimate.

Estimates of the average annual increase of the unauthorized population for the latest period (1996–2000) show dramatic growth, higher even than the extraordinary growth related to IRCA (as estimated by Warren for 1988 through 1992). However, at least some of the increase might be a reflection of better coverage of the U.S. population in the 2000 CPS. Estimates for March 2001, a date not as subject to coverage improvements due to Census outreach, indicate that the unauthorized Mexican immigrant population had reached 4.5 million, implying an average annual increase of 400,000 Mexican immigrants between 1996 and 2001.[7]

Table 4.3 presents estimates of various measures of annual international migration to the United States based on the CPS and administrative data from the INS. The first column, based on CPS data

---

[7]Based on the difference between estimates of the Mexican unauthorized immigrant population developed by Bean et al. (2001) and Bean, Van Hook, and Woodrow-Lafield (2001). The low estimate of this population for 2001 suggests an average annual increase of about 180,000 between 1996 and 2001, whereas the high estimate places the annual average increase at about 650,000.

## Table 4.3

### Average Annual Flow of Migrants to the United States, 1980–2000

| Time Period | International Migrants | Noncitizen International Migrants | Persons Given Legal Permanent Residency | Newly Admitted Legal Permanent Residents | Temporary Migrants |
|---|---|---|---|---|---|
| 1980–1984 | 978,640 | | 571,665 | | |
| 1986–1990 | 1,271,520 | | 620,257 | 392,066 | 264,581 |
| 1990–1994 | 1,305,081 | 809,150 | 777,512 | 487,423 | 563,958 |
| 1995–1999 | 1,318,393 | 856,955 | 764,799 | 382,441 | 785,405 |
| 1995–2000 | 1,401,014 | 910,659 | | | |

SOURCE: Authors' tabulations based on CPS and INS data.

for location of residence one year prior to the survey, suggests that the number of international migrants, including both U.S. citizens and noncitizens, was consistently high during the 1990s. The second column indicates that the flow of noncitizen migrants increased in the latter half of the 1990s.[8] At the same time, the number of people granted legal permanent residency and the number of newly admitted permanent residents (many of whom were already living in the United States and had simply returned home to apply for a visa) declined between 1995 and 1999. Temporary migration increased substantially in the late 1990s. These data, as well as those presented in Table 4.2, suggest that the number of unauthorized immigrants to the United States might have been higher in the late 1990s than it was in the early 1990s. However, the magnitude of the difference depends on the extent to which temporary migrants were captured in the CPS. If temporary migrants were not captured there, then the increase in the number represents an actual increase in the unauthorized population, but if they were captured, the increase in the unauthorized population may not be as large in the latter part of the 1990s. In any event, we do not find evidence that the flow of unauthorized immigrants declined substantially in the late 1990s.

---

[8]The increase in 1995–1999 was less substantial than that in 1995–2000, due perhaps to the coverage issue or to a large one-year increase between 1999 and 2000.

# Immigration Flows: Estimates from Mexican Data

In this section, we examine patterns of migration to the United States using national and subnational surveys of the Mexican population. We focus on Mexico because many immigrants from Mexico are unauthorized at the time of crossing, and because a majority of the new unauthorized immigrants come from Mexico. Unfortunately, the Mexican Census of 2000 does not include information about the legal status of those who had migrated to the United States. However, the 1992 INEGI survey showed that the overwhelming majority of those migrants (about 4 of every 5) were unauthorized. Warren (2000) has estimated that almost 70 percent of new unauthorized entrants to the United States are from Mexico. Thus, overall trends in the number of migrants from Mexico almost certainly reflect trends in unauthorized migration from Mexico and are an important determinant of unauthorized immigration to the United States.

Data gathered in the United States on Mexican immigrants and data gathered in Mexico on Mexicans in the United States are not completely compatible. Migrants surveyed in Mexico are more likely to be short-term or recent migrants to the United States than are those included in the U.S. data. That is, Mexicans who have resided in the United States for many years are less likely to be a part of a household in Mexico than are those who have recently departed.[9] Furthermore, the INEGI data provide information about the number of people who made at least one trip to the United States over the past five years, while the CPS tabulations are estimates of Mexicans in the United States at any one time.

We use data from the 1992 and 1997 INEGI national surveys and the Mexican 2000 Census. These data include information on household members who have migrated to the United States. We look at migration within five years, two years, and one year prior to the survey year. We also look at the number of migrants who had returned to Mexico by the time of the survey.

---

[9]Unlike the U.S. Census Bureau's definition of a household (all people living in a housing unit), INEGI allows that some members of a household might not be residents in the household.

Use of data from the INEGI surveys and the Mexican 2000 Census leads to different results, depending on the time period considered. As shown in Figure 4.2, the total number of members of Mexican households who had made at least one trip to the United States was substantially lower between 1995 and 2000 than it was in either of the two preceding five-year intervals. This decline was experienced by both men and women (not shown). However, the number of Mexicans who remained in the United States was higher at the time of the 2000 Census than it was in 1992, although still lower than the number in 1997. Thus, while fewer people made at least one trip to the United States in the most recent period, the number who stayed in the United States was relatively high. These results correspond to our findings in the previous chapter.

The estimates of migration from Mexico for more-recent emigrants show a slightly different pattern than those for the five-year migrants. In

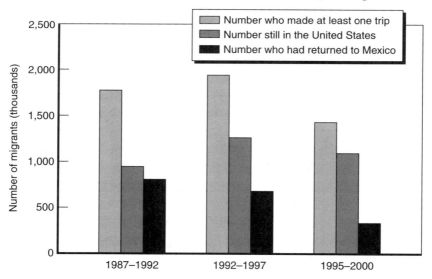

SOURCES: Authors' tabulations of 1992 and 1997 ENADID and Mexican 2000 Census data.

**Figure 4.2—Number of Mexicans 15 Years of Age and Older Who Went to the United States in the Past Five Years**

particular, as shown in Figure 4.3, the number of Mexican household members who left for the United States within the previous year was about the same in 2000 as it was in 1997, and in both years the flows were higher than they were in 1992.[10] In addition, the number who had left Mexico in the past one or two years *and* remained in the United States was much larger in 2000 and 1997 than it was in 1992. These numbers might provide a more accurate picture of trends just prior to the survey date because of better recall and because there is likely to be less subjectivity about whether recent emigrants are considered household members.

These estimates from the Mexican 2000 Census and surveys are not wholly consistent with the estimates developed from the CPS. It is

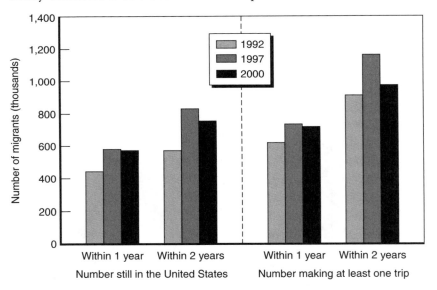

SOURCES: Authors' tabulations of 1992 and 1997 ENADID and Mexican 2000 Census data.

**Figure 4.3—Number of Mexicans 15 Years of Age and Older Who Went to the United States Within One and Two Years of the Survey Date**

---

[10]As discussed earlier, the net effect of migration from Mexico to the United States depends on how long the migrants stay in the United States.

possible, perhaps probable, that the two data sources capture different migrant populations. The U.S. data miss short-term and cyclical migrants who are captured in the Mexican data, and the Mexican data miss long-term and permanent migrants who appear in the U.S. data. Still, data from both sides of the border suggest that the number of migrants from Mexico who stay in the United States long enough to be included in the U.S. data was relatively high in the late 1990s.

## Labor Market Evidence: Farm Workers

Although the number of unauthorized immigrants in the United States is at an all-time high, it is possible that increased border enforcement has kept the numbers from being even higher. One way to test this possibility is by examining the supply of unauthorized workers in the U.S. labor market. Unauthorized immigrants tend to be concentrated in various low-skill occupations. A restriction in the supply of unauthorized workers relative to demand should be apparent in data on the number of low-skill workers, their wages, and their unemployment rates. An increase in the number of low-skill workers is not in itself sufficient evidence that increased border enforcement has not worked: The number of low-skill workers might have increased even more had it not been for increased enforcement. However, changes in the number of low-skill workers in conjunction with changes in their wages and unemployment rates should indicate whether the demand for low-skill workers has outpaced the supply. Increased border enforcement might have restricted the supply of such workers, while the economic boom of the late 1990s might have led to an increase in the demand for them.

We focus on one particular occupation in depth, farm workers, for two reasons:[11] Unauthorized immigrants are likely to be more heavily concentrated in farm work than in other sectors of the labor market, and we have a wealth of data on farm workers. In fact, one survey of U.S.

---

[11]A full treatment of our labor-force findings can be found in a PPIC Working Paper, "Has Increased Border Enforcement Tightened U.S. Labor Markets?" by Hans P. Johnson (2002). That paper includes a detailed examination of low-skill labor markets for farm workers as well as an examination of labor markets for other low-skill occupations.

farm workers includes a question on legal status. If border enforcement has substantially reduced the flow of unauthorized immigrants, we would expect to see a significant effect among farm workers.

Our analysis of farm workers suggests that border enforcement may have limited the increase in unauthorized immigrant workers, but the evidence of such an effect is weak at best. We observe small wage increases among farm workers in the late 1990s and falling unemployment rates. However, the increases in wages are about the same or even less than those in other occupations. The strong U.S. economy could explain the wage rate and unemployment rate patterns observed. The supply of low-skill Mexican workers increased substantially. Most important, we find a substantial increase in the number of unauthorized farm workers. Table 4.4 summarizes these findings.

Data on farm workers are relatively abundant: The National Agricultural Workers Survey (NAWS), the National Agricultural Statistics Service (NASS), and the March CPS all provide national information on farm workers. In California, the Employment Development Department (EDD) provides California-specific estimates.[12] We use all of these data sources to examine the effect of increased border enforcement on the agricultural sector.

Table 4.4

Summary of Labor-Force Findings for Farm Workers

| Measure | Outcome |
| --- | --- |
| Number of workers | Little change overall; large increase in unauthorized workers. |
| Wages | Increase in last few years. |
| Unemployment rates | Decline. |
| Other indicators | Some recent declines in the difference between seasonal peak and seasonal trough employment. |

[12]For more information on these data sources, see Appendix A.

Nationally, the total number of farm workers changed little in the 1990s, after a substantial decline from the 1970s. This pattern is generally observed across several datasets, including, for example, the NASS, a survey of farm-worker employers.[13]

We also explore whether the number of *unauthorized* farm workers has changed. Data from the NAWS provide information on the composition of farm workers, including legal status.[14] As shown in Figure 4.4, the proportion of unauthorized farm workers has increased dramatically from 1988 to 1998. Even if we include currently legal but previously unauthorized immigrants (persons granted amnesty under IRCA) with currently unauthorized immigrants in the late 1980s, we still see substantial increases during the 1990s. Most of the increases occurred between 1988 and 1996; since then, they have slowed

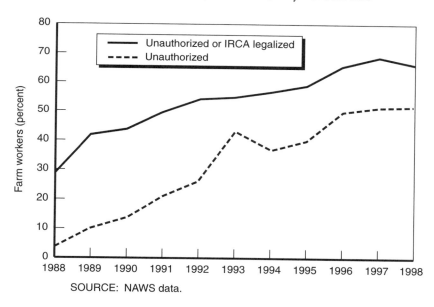

SOURCE: NAWS data.

Figure 4.4—Farm Workers by Legal Status, 1988–1998 (Update)

[13]We use the NASS numbers of "hired workers," which include farm workers but do not include workers in agricultural services working on farms.

[14]Documentation is self-reported, which suggests that unauthorized migrants are underreported.

considerably. Still, according to the NAWS, over half of the nation's farm workers in 1998 were unauthorized immigrants. Recent estimates place the proportion of unauthorized farm workers even higher, at 58 percent (Martin, 2002).[15]

The proportion of *recent* unauthorized immigrants has also increased. Coupled with the previous estimates of trends in the number of farm workers, the NAWS data suggest that the number of unauthorized farm workers increased dramatically during the 1990s, and that much of the increase was concurrent with increases in border enforcement.

## Summary

According to estimates developed by several researchers, the number of unauthorized immigrants in the United States is higher now than it has ever been. With at least 7 million and possibly more than 9 million unauthorized immigrants living in the United States, this population is perhaps twice as large as it was prior to the legalization program of the late 1980s. The number of unauthorized farm workers actually increased with the border enforcement build-up.

Determining the annual flow of unauthorized immigrants is difficult and involves considerable uncertainty. Data from the United States suggest that the flows in the late 1990s were quite high despite the intensification of border enforcement. Data from Mexico also suggest large flows of Mexican immigrants to the United States in the latter part of the 1990s. Overall, the picture is one of a large and rapidly growing population of unauthorized immigrants in the United States.

---

[15]This is a "projected" figure.

# 5. Has the Build-up Changed the Way People Cross the Border?

In this chapter, we analyze changes in behavior associated with border crossing—manner of crossing, crossing place, probability of apprehension, and use of smugglers—that could be attributed to the border build-up. We analyze data from the INS, EMIF (*Encuesta Nacional sobre Migración en la Frontera Norte de México*), ENADID, and the MMP.

We find that the build-up may have changed the manner in which people cross the U.S.-Mexican border and increased the probability of apprehension. Immigrants are crossing at different places, and smugglers, known as coyotes, have become indispensable. In addition to increasing the cost of hiring a coyote, the build-up appears to be increasing the risks of dying at the border.

## Crossing Places and Apprehensions

One of the goals of the border build-up is to reroute crossers from traditional, urban areas to less-accessible and less-populated crossing sites. This goal has been achieved. As the INS concentrates its efforts in particular border cities, migrants cross at less-guarded areas to decrease the likelihood of being apprehended (Orrenius, 2002). Figure 5.1 shows the number of apprehensions at different crossing places for 1992, 1995, 1998, and 2001. These figures indicate a shift in crossing locations. When Operation Gatekeeper in San Diego was implemented in 1994, the number of apprehensions declined in San Diego and increased in El Centro. Similarly, when Operation Hold-the-Line was implemented in El Paso in 1993, apprehensions declined in El Paso and increased in other Texas and Arizona locations.

Although the build-up led to a shift in crossing locations from more- to less-populated areas, the total number of apprehensions did not begin

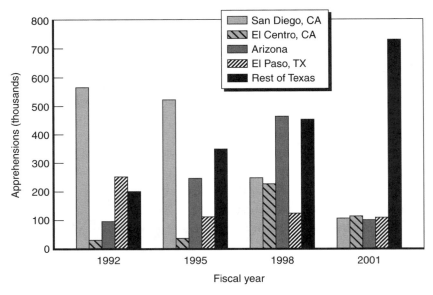

SOURCE: INS border statistics.

**Figure 5.1—U.S. Border Patrol Apprehensions on the Southwest Border**

to decline until 2001 (Figure 5.2). This decline may be an indication of the success of the build-up; however, it could also be the result of declining economic opportunities in 2001 and the events of September 11 (Smith and Ellingwood, 2001; Cornelius, 2001).

Using the MMP data, we find that the probability of apprehension declined from the 1970s until the early 1990s (Figure 5.3). Coinciding with the increase in border enforcement is an abrupt increase in the proportion of immigrants who were apprehended.[1] Whereas about 15 percent of male household heads in the MMP sample were apprehended in 1992, more than one-third of those who moved in 1998 were apprehended.

---

[1]Donato (2002) also finds an increase in the probability of apprehension during the period of increased enforcement. She finds increasing differences for men and women, with women being more likely to be apprehended.

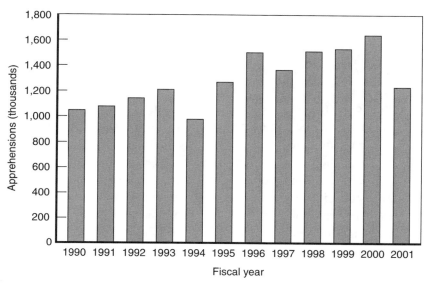

SOURCE: INS apprehension data.

Figure 5.2—Total Apprehensions on the Southwest Border

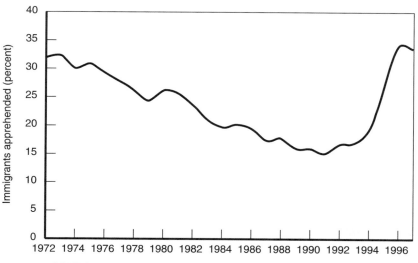

SOURCE: Authors' calculations from the MMP migration file. Results are presented as three-year moving averages.

Figure 5.3—Proportion of Unauthorized Immigrants Who Have Been Apprehended

Some authors argue that as the border becomes more difficult to cross, prospective migrants stay in border cities longer. This longer stay, in turn, may eventually deter some immigrants from crossing (Orrenius, 2001). We looked at both the MMP and the EMIF sample for indications of a shift in migration from international to domestic migration or increases in the length of time immigrants spend in cities along the border. We find no evidence of a shift from international to domestic migration, but we do see an increase in the proportion of migrants who choose Baja California as their place of destination (Figure 5.4). However, without modeling, it is impossible to determine whether this is due to an increase in border enforcement or a strong and rapidly growing border economy. Our surveys also indicate that since the border enforcement build-up, people do indeed stay longer in border regions before crossing.

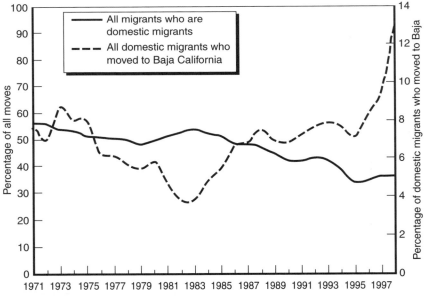

SOURCE: Authors' calculations from the MMP person file. Results are presented as three-year moving averages.

Figure 5.4—Proportion of Migrants in the MMP Sample Who Moved
Domestically

# Coyotes

In general, the build-up has increased the demand for smugglers (coyotes), the costs associated with crossing, and the power the coyotes have over potential migrants (Andreas, 2001; Spener, 2001). More immigrants are using coyotes now than in previous years (Figure 5.5). Their use increased from 1972 until 1981 and then remained at 70 percent from 1981 until 1993. A significant increase in the use of coyotes overlaps with the onset of the stepped-up enforcement. By 1997, 89 percent of unauthorized immigrants hired a smuggler to cross the U.S.-Mexican border.

As the INS expected, the cost of hiring a coyote has increased dramatically since the build-up (Cornelius, 2002; INS, 1997b). In our interviews, we learned that the cost depends on the starting point, crossing location, and U.S. destination. For most people, crossing from Tijuana to Los Angeles in 2000 cost about $800, but the price rose to about $2,000 if the crossing involved passing through a checkpoint. For

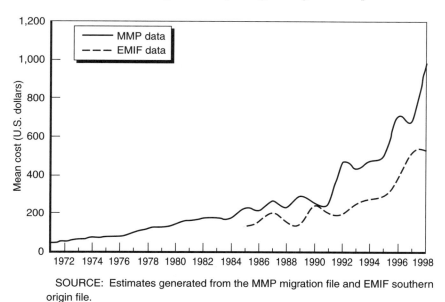

SOURCE: Estimates generated from the MMP migration file and EMIF southern origin file.

Figure 5.5—Proportion of Household Head Migrants Who Used a Coyote

those who made arrangements with a coyote from their home town, the fee was about $1,500. Some interviewees from Central America paid as much as $5,500 to reach Los Angeles.

Figure 5.6 presents two estimates of the mean cost of hiring a coyote. Both samples show a sizable increase in this cost starting in the mid 1990s. The MMP data indicate that the cost of hiring a coyote increased from close to $500 in 1993 to about $1,000 in 1998. The cost of hiring a coyote at the border is lower, as illustrated by the results from the EMIF data; but even there, the cost increased from close to $200 in 1993 to $700 in 1998.

Our interviews in Mexico and the United States indicate that people-smuggling is becoming a complex and profitable industry. In many cases, one person will make an agreement with the migrant or the migrant's family. The parties agree on a price, pick-up and drop-off places, and the form of payment. Most of the interviewees had relatives in the United States who paid the fee when the migrant arrived at a family member's house in the United States. Those without connections

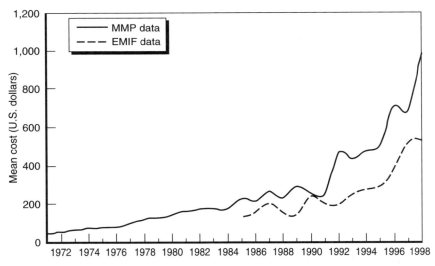

SOURCE: Estimates generated from the MMP migration file and EMIF southern origin file.

**Figure 5.6—Estimated Coyote Costs**

in the United States had to pay in advance or personally upon arrival. Because these people had to carry money with them, they were more vulnerable to robbery, sometimes by the coyote. For the most part, the person who made the arrangement was not the same person who transported the migrants. In many cases, coyotes hire "guides" to lead people across the U.S. border. Yet another person may take the migrant once he or she has crossed the border to the U.S. destination. The few people we spoke with from Central America said that numerous guides and coyotes could be involved in their journey from their home towns to their U.S. destinations. A day laborer in Los Angeles explained:

> There are coyotes that bring you the contract . . . from Central America . . . Costa Ricans, Nicaraguans, Salvadorians, Hondurans . . . and they get everyone together in one city. . . . They might take two hundred people, then they say, "This is a contract to California"; then this guy leaves you with another guy, and then with another . . . yes, until they get you here. The one here is in charge of getting you to your destination that you're going to . . . and you have to give him the money. (Los Angeles)

From the EMIF data, we can see that migrants are not only more likely to cross with coyotes, but they are also less likely to move alone. There has been a decline in the proportion of migrants who move alone, and an increasing proportion are moving with five or more people (Figure 5.7). This pattern is also corroborated by the MMP data, which indicate that only 24 percent of the household heads in the sample moved alone after the build-up, compared with 40 percent in the 1987–1994 period.

## Summary

The build-up has affected the manner in which people cross the U.S.-Mexican border; in particular, immigrants are crossing the border in rural, more dangerous places. The build-up has also increased the probability of apprehension. Nevertheless, the number of apprehensions declined for the first time in many years in 2001. This might be partly due to the new border strategy, but the downturn in the U.S. economy and the events of September 11 may have also reduced the number of people attempting to cross. Furthermore, smugglers have become both more necessary for border crossings and more expensive.

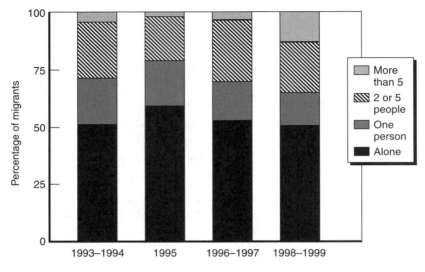

SOURCE: Authors' calculations from EMIF 1993–1999 data.

**Figure 5.7—Number of People with Whom Migrants Cross**

# 6. Has Increased Border Enforcement Affected Border Deaths?

The Border Patrol's efforts have resulted in unauthorized migrants choosing longer, more hazardous routes. Another result of this strategy has been a shift in the primary causes and places of migrant deaths. Using a combination of data sources, we find that deaths of unauthorized migrants declined in the early 1990s, reaching their low point in the years immediately preceding the increase in border enforcement. Following the introduction of the Border Patrol's strategy, however, migrant deaths increased rapidly, reaching their highest peak in 15 years in FY 2000.

The number of border deaths is determined by the number of crossers and the risk of dying during any given crossing. Fewer deaths do not necessarily mean a decline in the hazard, and vice versa. Although there is no data source with precise figures on the annual number of unauthorized crossings, we use apprehension data to show that the likelihood of dying appears to be increasing. As deaths increasingly occur in remote locations, the number of unrecorded deaths may also have gone up over time. The rise in deaths is attributable, at least in part, to the increased danger of longer, more difficult crossings.

## Migrant Deaths at the Border

The subject of migrant deaths has begun to receive critical attention from the media and researchers. Local and national newspapers frequently provide accounts of the risks unauthorized immigrants take in coming to the United States: trekking through the Imperial Valley desert in 115-degree weather, swimming across the All-American Canal, and the multiple-day hike over mountain ranges during winter (Sanchez,

1999; Associated Press, 2000; Navarro, 2001; Booth, 2000). In addition, several studies in recent years have examined the frequency, causes, and locations of migrant deaths (Eschbach et al., 1999; Cornelius, 2001; Eschbach, Hagan, and Rodriguez, 2001; GAO, 2001).

Such studies rely on several datasets, each with its own limitations. Most published statistics probably undercount the number of deaths, because some bodies are never found. In addition, most organizations that track migrant deaths have only recently begun to do so systematically, making it difficult to describe pre- and post-enforcement trends. Also, these datasets often do not include bodies found on the Mexican side of the border.[1]

The first academic study to analyze longitudinal data was conducted by the Center for Immigration Research (CIR) at the University of Houston. The authors collected data on the deaths of probable migrants from local medical investigators' and examiners' offices in California, Arizona, and New Mexico and from vital registration records in Texas. Additional data were collected from press reports of drowned bodies recovered by Mexican officials along a portion of the Texas border. CIR documented over 1,600 possible migrant fatalities between 1993 and 1997. The report concluded that while there were not substantially more fatalities in 1997 than in 1993, there were shifts in the causes of deaths, due in part to the more hazardous routes taken by crossers. Migrant deaths from environmental causes increased fivefold during this period, while deaths from auto–pedestrian accidents decreased by roughly two-thirds (Eschbach et al., 1999). Because more of the border crossings in recent years are occurring in rural areas, bodies are less likely to be found.

Using data collected by the Mexican Ministry of Foreign Relations (MMFR), Cornelius documented 1,422 migrant deaths along the Southwest border from 1996 to 2000, with 35 percent of the deaths occurring in 2000 alone (Cornelius, 2001). In addition to stressing that a large proportion of the deaths occurred recently, Cornelius highlighted the increasing likelihood of dying from environmental factors. In 1995, MMFR data documented five unauthorized immigrant deaths from hypothermia, dehydration, or heat stroke along the California-Mexican

---

[1] For a more detailed description of these data sources, see Appendix A.

border. In the first 10 and one-half months of 2000, 80 unauthorized immigrants died from those causes (Cornelius, 2001). Like the CIR study, Cornelius presents data on migrant deaths that occurred after much of the increase in border enforcement and is therefore unable to comment on how trends in the post-enforcement period differ from those before the build-up.

In March 2001, CIR released the first report that compares pre- and post-enforcement trends in migrant deaths, documenting probable unauthorized migrant deaths from 1985 to 1998. Researchers used the vital registration system of the United States, the only dataset that systematically tracked deaths during both periods of enforcement. Several trends emerge from these data. As would be expected, the number of deaths in a given year is highly correlated with the flow of unauthorized immigrants for that year. Thus, we see that the number of migrant deaths fell during the beginning of the 1990s and increased again in the mid 1990s. The lowest number of migrant deaths occurred in the years immediately preceding the border enforcement increase. After the new enforcement strategy was implemented, deaths began to rise (see Table 6.1).

The most dramatic trend has been the increase in deaths due to environmental factors. In 1993 and 1994, the early years of the border build-up, only six documented deaths each year were due to environmental causes. CIR data indicate that in 1998, 84 people died from environmental causes. The reduction in auto–pedestrian deaths offers another indication that the flow of unauthorized migration shifted from urban to rural areas. The number of deaths from drowning, after decreasing in the mid 1990s, rose to its highest annual level in 1998. Homicide deaths dropped significantly over the entire period, a factor that had a large effect on the total number of deaths. As part (a) of Figure 6.1 shows, the causes of death associated with a more difficult crossing—environmental, drowning, or unknown reason—have been rising since the mid 1990s. As part (b) of the figure indicates, deaths from other causes—those associated with more-urban areas—are less likely to occur in the post-enforcement period.

## Table 6.1

## Migrant Deaths Reported by Vital Registration System, 1985–1998

| Year | Train | Motor Vehicle | Auto–Pedestrian | Environmental | Unknown | Drowning | Homicide | All Other | Total Deaths |
|---|---|---|---|---|---|---|---|---|---|
| 1985 | 14 | 47 | 32 | 33 | 40 | 67 | 69 | 13 | 301 |
| 1986 | 16 | 33 | 40 | 24 | 38 | 75 | 71 | 13 | 294 |
| 1987 | 15 | 56 | 47 | 9 | 35 | 77 | 62 | 17 | 303 |
| 1988 | 11 | 60 | 56 | 11 | 43 | 71 | 73 | 30 | 344 |
| 1989 | 4 | 49 | 47 | 8 | 27 | 64 | 47 | 19 | 261 |
| 1990 | 7 | 50 | 48 | 10 | 26 | 53 | 56 | 9 | 252 |
| 1991 | 9 | 35 | 43 | 11 | 18 | 51 | 64 | 9 | 231 |
| 1992 | 13 | 37 | 32 | 6 | 20 | 60 | 41 | 11 | 207 |
| 1993 | 6 | 29 | 26 | 6 | 21 | 49 | 35 | 7 | 173 |
| 1994 | 6 | 36 | 22 | 9 | 23 | 48 | 27 | 6 | 171 |
| 1995 | 17 | 51 | 13 | 19 | 32 | 56 | 31 | 4 | 206 |
| 1996 | 18 | 40 | 18 | 44 | 34 | 40 | 25 | 9 | 210 |
| 1997 | 7 | 53 | 17 | 54 | 35 | 68 | 27 | 2 | 256 |
| 1998 | 17 | 41 | 17 | 84 | 40 | 81 | 20 | 3 | 286 |
| All | 160 | 617 | 458 | 328 | 432 | 860 | 648 | 152 | 3,495 |

SOURCE: Assembled from CIR data.

Data collected by the Border Patrol show similar trends. These data are restricted to bodies actually found by or reported to Border Patrol agents on the U.S. side of the border. Unfortunately, the data cannot show the effect of the current strategy upon migrant deaths over time, as the Border Patrol did not systematically collect aggregate data along the border until FY 1998. The INS reported 261 migrant deaths along the border in FY 1998, 236 deaths in FY 1999, 367 deaths in FY 2000, and 330 in FY 2001. Fifty-five migrant deaths have been reported in the first five months of FY 2002. Because the last seven months of the fiscal year include the summer months, when a higher percentage of deaths occur, the number of deaths in FY 2002 is expected to surpass that in FY 1998 and FY 1999. The most common reasons for death reported by the Border Patrol were environmental: drowning and exposure (Table 6.2). Although the INS data cannot be used to show the effect of increased enforcement upon migrant deaths, the data are consistent with the CIR findings that a large number of migrants are dying from environmental causes.

## a. Environmental causes

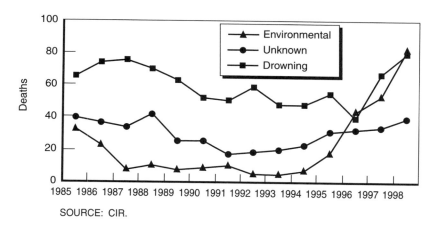

SOURCE: CIR.

## b. Other causes

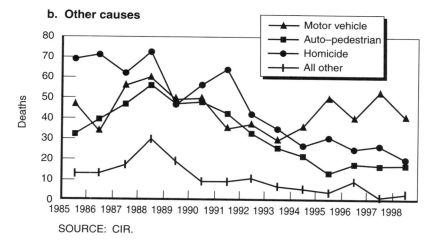

SOURCE: CIR.

Figure 6.1—Deaths of Foreign Transients Due to Selected Causes,
1985–1998

69

## Table 6.2

### Migrant Deaths, by Cause of Death, FY 1998–2001[a]

| Cause of Death | 1998 | 1999 | 2000 | 2001[a] | Total | Percentage |
|---|---|---|---|---|---|---|
| Exposure to heat | 87 | 57 | 135 | 27 | 306 | 30 |
| Drowning | 89 | 72 | 92 | 40 | 293 | 29 |
| Unknown | 29 | 38 | 43 | 45 | 155 | 15 |
| Motor vehicle accident | 16 | 21 | 48 | 22 | 107 | 11 |
| Other | 16 | 15 | 27 | 10 | 68 | 7 |
| Exposure to cold | 16 | 18 | 17 | 4 | 55 | 5 |
| Train | 8 | 14 | 5 | 1 | 28 | 3 |
| Confined space | 0 | 1 | 0 | 0 | 1 | <1 |
| Total | 261 | 236 | 367 | 149 | 1,013 | 100 |

SOURCES: Border Patrol; GAO.

[a]Through June 1, 2001.

In Figure 6.2, we use INS Border Patrol data to complete the trend established by CIR data. Although the datasets are not identical, both include bodies found by or reported to officials on the U.S. side of the border. Data are available from both datasets for 1998, and in that year, the difference between the two is small, i.e., 22 deaths.[2] Unauthorized migrant deaths decreased during the post-IRCA period but rose during the introduction of the new border enforcement strategy. Migrant deaths reached a 15-year peak in FY 2000, the most recent year for which we have complete data.

As mentioned earlier, the number of deaths is a function of the hazard rate and the flow of unauthorized migration for a given year. Although apprehension data are not a proxy for migration flow data, they can be useful for describing trends in migrant deaths. Since the implementation of the new Border Patrol strategy, there has been a steady increase in the number of deaths per 100,000 apprehensions (Figure 6.3). In 1993, there were 11.9 deaths per 100,000

---

[2]We have subtracted the number of homicides from the CIR data because INS data do not include homicide victims.

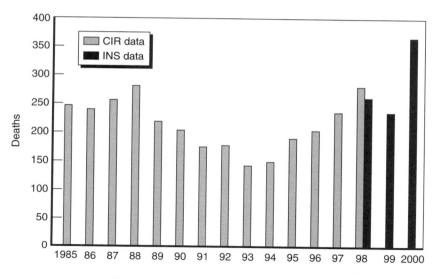

Figure 6.2—Reported Migrant Deaths

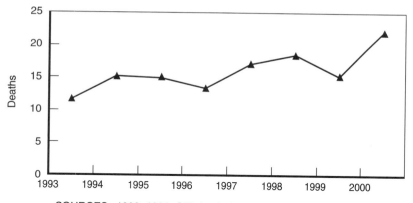

SOURCES: 1993–1998, CIR death data; 1999–2000, INS death data; 1993–2000, INS apprehension data.

Figure 6.3—Migrant Deaths per 100,000 Apprehensions

apprehensions; by FY 2000, that number had risen to 15.4 deaths. Again, this figure may underestimate the number of deaths, as bodies of migrants who died in recent years may be less likely to be found due to increased crossing at more-remote locations.

## Border Safety Initiative

In response to increased concerns over migrant deaths near the border, the INS implemented the Border Safety Initiative (BSI) in June 1998. The program is a coordinated effort with Mexican officials that focuses on prevention, search and rescue, and identification. Under the BSI, the Border Patrol has issued public safety awareness campaigns on television and radio, equipped Border Patrol vehicles with additional first-aid kits and safety devices, and intensified surveillance in hazardous areas. The INS pledged to intensify safety efforts in June 2000 by ensuring safety training for all Border Patrol officers along the Southwest border.

According to the INS, Border Patrol agents saved more than 2,000 immigrants from life-threatening situations during the first two years of the Safety Initiative (INS, 2000). In the most recent fiscal year for which we have complete data (FY 2000), agents rescued almost 2,500 migrants (Rooney, 2001). While the BSI has successfully reduced the number of migrant deaths, its success suggests a substantial increase in the number of perilous journeys undertaken over the last few years. This increase is partially attributable to the redirection of points of entry but may also suggest an increase in the flow of unauthorized migrants.

Many nongovernmental organizations have pledged their support to migrants who attempt the more perilous trips. Spurred by reports of migrant deaths due to dehydration, several citizens of Arizona recently put up water stations in the desert for thirsty migrants (Fox, 2000).

## Ranchers

As noted earlier, more unauthorized migrants now cross the border in rural sectors. The Tucson sector, for example, accounted for 7 percent of all apprehensions in the first half of FY 1993, compared with 19 percent of all apprehensions in the first half of FY 1997 (GAO, 1997a).

During FY 1998, the Tucson sector surpassed San Diego as the busiest crossing point for unauthorized migrants (based on apprehensions), and by FY 1999 the total number of apprehensions in that sector was more than twice the number five years before (Janofsky, 2000).

Migrants crossing through the Tucson sector frequently pass through private property owned by Arizona ranchers. Angered by large numbers of migrants trespassing on their land, a small number of these ranchers have been patrolling their property and detaining suspected illegal immigrants at gunpoint until Border Patrol agents come to pick them up. Roger Barnett, a rancher from Douglas, Arizona, testified before the U.S. Congress that in the span of one year, he and his brothers turned over more than 1,000 unauthorized migrants to the Border Patrol (U.S. House of Representatives, 1999).

As more ranchers take up arms to defend their property, concerns have arisen over human rights abuses. Mexico's Secretary of Foreign Affairs, Rosario Green, announced in May 2000 that the government of Mexico had plans to file suit in U.S. Federal Court against Arizona ranchers who have injured unauthorized workers. Green stated that in one 16-month period, U.S. citizens committed 32 incidents of violence against unauthorized Mexican workers, resulting in seven injuries and two deaths ("Injured Mexican Immigrants Will File Suit," 2000). A few days later, at the 17th annual meeting of the U.S.-Mexico Binational Commission, Secretary Green reiterated the Mexican government's commitment to the investigation and punishment of human rights violations by U.S. citizens and announced that U.S. Attorney General Reno pledged her support (U.S.-Mexico Binational Commission, 2000).

As tensions between ranchers and human rights groups have risen, several calls have been made for help from the United Nations. In May 2000, Mexico's National Human Rights Commission submitted a formal request to the United Nations to investigate allegations of violence against Mexican laborers by U.S. citizens (Lellingwood and Schrader, 2000). Later that month, a United Nations special envoy for immigration issues met with Secretary Green and Arizona Governor Jane Hull to investigate claims of abuse (Reuters, 2000). In response to requests by the California Rural Legal Assistance Foundation, the American Civil Liberties Union, and the Mexican government, Mary

Robinson, the United Nations High Commissioner for Human Rights, toured the border in November 1999 to gather information on the deaths of immigrants trying to cross it (Sanchez, 1999). To date, the United Nations has not released a formal recommendation.

## Immigrants' Experiences at the Border

Our respondents reported that the build-up has increased the danger at the border. The interviews revealed three different types of danger:

- Dying while crossing the desert, mountains, or river,
- Being assaulted, attacked, or killed by robbers, or
- Being raped, abused, mistreated, or left behind by the coyotes or their guides.

For instance, one migrant said:

> Those going through the desert die by dehydration and those crossing through the river drown. (Mexico)

A woman we spoke to in Mexico explained:

> Many are murdered while crossing; others drown. If you have to run, you do not even know in what direction because you do not know where you are. (Mexico)

Many respondents talked about being robbed by people hiding in tunnels or in the mountains or by corrupt Mexican policemen. Although they may perhaps not be representative of all Mexican migrants, our respondents mentioned many more cases of abuse by the Mexican police than by the Border Patrol. In general, the migrants we spoke with understood the job of the Border Patrol and described their experience with them as positive. However, some mentioned abuses by the INS:

> The government on that side monitors the border, and the patrols are very abusive. I have seen how the patrols treated three young people badly using dogs. The patrols on this side are also very abusive and steal from people attempting to cross. I once heard a policeman talking to another one about how he had killed a young man to take his 700 pesos. (Mexico)

For the most part immigrants spoke about abuses by the Mexican *municipales* or the *judiciales*:

When the Mexicali police caught us, they took everything we had. If we had a necklace, they would take it from us. One time we were there and they took us in the patrol cars and told us, "You're going to jail for wanting to cross over the line and we are going to take you away, and you're going to pay a $500 fine for wanting to cross." That was the experience every time we went and came back from Mexico. (Los Angeles)

The U.S. patrol agents are better than the Mexican patrol. The Mexicans are the ones that treat people rather badly. Once, Mexican agents found us trying to cross and started to follow us. We decided that we were better off getting captured at the other side by the U.S. patrol.

People also talked about the increased difficulty of passing through treacherous terrain and spending numerous days in inhospitable places. Most spent a few days trying to cross, and many reported multiple crossing attempts. Some recounted sleeping in the mountains for days, running for hours on end, or going for long periods without food or water. Many described the experience as one of the most difficult in their life. In responding to a question about changes at the border, one migrant said:

Oh, much more difficult, because they've put up barriers, and with all that there is much more danger. When you arrive at the border and there they ask you, "Where are you going?" and there are many dishonest people, many who rob, many who attack you just to take the little money you have, and since you can no longer cross the line at Tijuana, you have to go through the desert, where you have to walk three or four or six days and sometimes even more. . . . And in the desert you run out of water, of food, of everything, because you can't carry much, because of the distance. The safer routes are longer, you have to walk longer and although it's safer it's uglier, with more desert. And the heat is intense, and the water runs out. Even if you take a gallon of water, since they come in those plastic gallon jugs, it gets hot, like soup, and it's useless. . . . It's useless. And when it is the cold season, it's very cold, and the whole time you go on struggling, and suffering. (Madera)

## Summary

Migrant deaths declined in the late 1980s and early 1990s, reaching a low point in the years immediately preceding the increase in border enforcement. Following the introduction of the Border Patrol's current enforcement strategy, which increased the difficulty and risk of crossing the border, migrant deaths increased rapidly, reaching a 15-year peak in FY 2000. At the same time, the INS Border Safety Initiative prevented a significant number of deaths. The increase in migrant deaths, coupled with the substantial number of life-saving rescues by the Border Patrol, indicates that crossing has become more difficult.

Unauthorized migrants are now more likely to die from environmental causes than ever before. The shift in causes of death is due to changing migration patterns. Multiple-day routes over rough terrain have taken the place of crossing by foot or automobile in urban areas. Evidence of the more difficult journey can be found both in the quantitative data and in the personal accounts of migrants.

# 7. What Are the Policy Options?

Crafting a successful immigration policy is a daunting task, one that must consider and balance the dynamics of international relations, the U.S. political climate, the push for free markets, the effects of recent terrorist events, and the legacy of past policies. The current strategy, which increases the difficulty and cost of entering the United States illegally, has not yet achieved its primary goal of "prevention through deterrence." The quantitative and anecdotal evidence in this report indicates that although the risks and costs involved in illegally entering the United States have increased, the number of unauthorized migrants in the United States has also increased. Moreover, the evidence indicates that unauthorized immigrants are taking longer and more-dangerous trips, paying more for them, suffering more deaths while crossing, and staying longer once they get here.

This chapter reviews some aspects of the current border enforcement strategy as well as other policy options. Its purpose is not to advocate specific policies but rather to examine the current policy in its context and to present some alternatives for controlling unauthorized immigration.

## The Border Build-up

The current border enforcement strategy has been in effect for more than eight years. During these years, border enforcement spending and the number of agents patrolling the border have both tripled. The first phase of the strategy called for deploying resources to the San Diego and El Paso sectors. In FY 1998, the INS began implementation of the second phase, reallocating resources to the Tucson and southern Texas sectors, which were experiencing higher numbers of unauthorized crossings. The INS does not consider the strategy to be fully implemented. As of August 2001, the INS estimated it would need an additional 3,200 to 5,500 Border Patrol agents, additional support personnel, and hundreds of millions of dollars in technological equipment and infrastructure for full implementation. It will take the INS at least five more years to achieve these goals (GAO, 2001). Full implementation of the strategy will also require reallocating agents to other sectors along the Southwest border and eventually to the sectors along the Canadian border and coastal waterways.

Although the strategy has achieved several of its secondary goals—a redirection of the flow of unauthorized crossings, an increase in the costs and risks of crossing, and an increase in the likelihood of apprehension—there is no evidence that the INS has achieved its primary goal of reducing both unauthorized crossings and the number of unauthorized persons living in the United States.

The terrorist attacks on New York and Washington on September 11, 2001, have both highlighted and changed the nature of the border enforcement policy discussion. Before the attacks, the United States and Mexico were moving toward a progressive bilateral agreement to legalize Mexican workers in the United States and to develop a safe, legal system for future migration. Since the attacks, the policy dialogue has shifted to border security, including an increase in the number of Border Patrol agents at both Canadian and Mexican entry points, more-stringent tracking systems for foreign visitors and temporary residents, and a thorough investigation of unauthorized immigrants currently living in the United States. The INS has made several policy changes to address the new threats posed by terrorism at crossing places.[1] It has also announced new visa restrictions that reduce the amount of time most tourists can stay in the United States from six months to 30 days, limit business travelers to six months, and require all foreign visitors wishing to

---

[1]In February 2002, the National Guard pledged 1,600 guardsmen to assist the INS and the Customs Service with inspections and crowd control along the northern and southern borders as well as at internal points of entry (Ibarra, 2002). Following President Bush's call to recruit additional Border Patrol agents, the INS announced plans to hire more than 2,000 new agents in FY 2002 and 2,000 more in FY 2003 (INS, 2002). The INS has addressed recent calls for increased security along the U.S.-Canadian border by sending several hundred Border Patrol agents north, providing additional boats and aircraft to patrol the Great Lakes, and making it more difficult to obtain Canadian boat landing permits, which allow holders to bypass U.S. Customs and immigration stations (Associated Press, 2002).

study in the United States to obtain an approved student visa before enrolling in coursework (Marquis, 2002).

Congress and the Bush Administration have also crafted new proposals. In January 2002, President Bush pledged an additional $2.1 billion to further increase security enforcement along the border and to develop a federal tracking system for monitoring the arrival and departure status of noncitizens (Allen and Miller, 2002). The Senate has agreed to postpone amnesty proposals for the moment and is instead debating the Enhanced Border Security and Visa Entry Reform Act of 2001, which would reduce the number of visas granted to citizens of countries that sponsor terrorism, make it more difficult to obtain student visas, and require federal agencies to implement a system of shared information that can better track immigrants' movements. Also as a fallout of September 11, the House of Representatives recently voted 405 to 9 to split the INS into two agencies, one presiding over enforcement of immigration laws, the other focusing on services to the immigrant population (McDonnell and Peterson, 2002). It is not clear how this split will affect the Southwest border strategy. While the current policy discussion has understandably focused on terrorist threats and national security, questions about unauthorized immigration as such have gone unanswered.

This report has focused on the effect of increased enforcement on the number and migration patterns of unauthorized immigrants. Strategies designed to prevent terrorists from entering the United States are, in some cases, the same strategies used to prevent unauthorized immigration—for example, visa background checks, tracking, and interior enforcement. However, the strategies differ in other respects. Identifying a terrorist requires much more information about a person's past than does identifying that person as an unauthorized worker.

By highlighting the need to identify everyone who enters the country, these national security concerns have altered the immigration policy debate. The current border strategy is to keep people out rather than to identify those who enter. Other policy options, such as regularizing unauthorized immigrant workers and creating a national identification card, have been discussed as policy alternatives to increased enforcement. In addition, Canada, Mexico, and the United States have been discussing a North American "security perimeter." Such a collaboration between the North American Free Trade Agreement (NAFTA) countries would facilitate the flow of commerce and people between the NAFTA partners, while harmonizing policies among members and increasing restrictions on nonmember countries (Meissner, 2001).

## The Policy Context: The Conflicting Mandate

Some experts have argued that the U.S. government has not prevented illegal immigration because of its conflicting mandate. Some groups demand strict enforcement, but labor-intensive industries—agriculture, apparel, construction, food processing, lodging, restaurant, and domestic help industries—demand a plentiful supply of workers. Some observers have suggested that the equilibrium level of enforcement emerges from the political pressures exerted on the government by both of these groups (Calavita, 1992, 1994; Hanson and Spilimbergo, 1999; Andreas, 2000). This conflict between those who advocate expanded immigration and those who plead for restrictions goes as far back as the mid 1880s, with the debate over Irish immigration (Higham, 1955; Cornelius, 1982).

IRCA tried to balance these conflicting mandates by legalizing a number of undocumented immigrants, imposing employer sanctions, allowing for additional farm workers to be admitted in case of labor shortages, and increasing border enforcement (Calavita, 1994). Many more immigrants than expected were legalized, and unauthorized immigration flows eventually increased to levels above those that existed before IRCA (Johnson, 1996; Calavita, 1994).

Part of the explanation for the failure of IRCA to decrease unauthorized immigration was that employer sanctions were never systematically enforced. The INS conducted very few inspections, and those few were performed randomly rather than focusing on the industries that were likely to hire undocumented immigrants (Bean, Vernez, and Keely, 1989). In addition, employers felt protected by the I-9 forms, as they were considered in compliance as long as they checked workers' papers. According to Calavita (1994):

Transforming the definition of compliance was crucial for eliminating employer opposition to the law. By simultaneously appeasing a public that demanded employer sanctions as well as employers who derived economic benefits from immigrant workers, the Simpson-Rodino bill proved to be a carefully crafted response to an underlying contradiction between political and economic forces. (p. 72)

As a consequence, only a few fines were levied on violators, and the amounts of the fines were small (Fix and Hill, 1990; Fix, 1991).

The nation now faces the same core question that has driven immigration debates and policies since the 19th century: How do we ensure a consistent flow of immigrant workers and simultaneously protect our national sovereignty by limiting the number of people entering the country? To address this question, we turn to the various policy options for decreasing unauthorized immigration; these options are summarized in Table 7.1, which also notes the advantages and disadvantages of each.[2]

## Increased Internal Enforcement

Border enforcement consists of policing land borders and ports of entry, while internal enforcement consists of traffic checkpoints, raids on worksites, and other internal patrols. Internal enforcement is politically difficult for the INS, due primarily to pressures from civil rights organizations as well as from employers of immigrants. The most controversial form of internal enforcement is the worksite raid. Calavita (1992) documents that the U.S. Border Patrol of El Paso issued orders to *stop* workplace enforcement during the agricultural harvests in the 1940s and 1950s. Recently, in 1998, the U.S. Attorney General, both Georgia senators, and three Georgia congressional representatives publicly criticized the INS for harming Georgia farmers after the INS conducted raids in the onion fields during the onion harvest (Hanson and Spilimbergo, 1999).

---

[2]For a more detailed examination of policy alternatives, see the U.S. Commission on Immigration Reform and Mexican Ministry of Foreign Affairs' Binational Study (U.S.-Mexico Binational Commission, 2000).

## Table 7.1

### Policy Options for Reducing Unauthorized Immigration

| Policy | Advantages | Disadvantages |
| --- | --- | --- |
| **Increase internal enforcement** | | |
| Inspect workplaces | Increases apprehensions; may deter unauthorized immigrants. | Employers dislike policy because they need workers; potential civil rights violations; profiling. |
| Target criminals | Leads to detention and deportation of criminal illegal immigrants; increases smuggling fees; may be useful for terrorism control. | Costly to detain so many immigrants; civil rights issues; excessive punishment for indefinite detentions; definition of deportable crimes may be too broad. |
| Expedited removal | Maximizes efficiency by not tying up court system. | No due process. |
| **Reduce employers' incentives** | | |
| Enforce labor laws | Worker protections; reduces incentives to exploit labor. | Hard to enforce; requires more personnel and resources. |
| Impose sanctions on employers who hire illegal immigrants | Holds employers accountable; discourages hiring unauthorized workers. | Politically difficult because it interrupts the flow of business; poor quality of INS data; targets foreign-born persons. |
| National identification card | Effectively determines legal status. | Extremely costly; privacy issues. |
| Guest-worker programs | Formalizes migration already taking place; safer than clandestine relationship. | Long bureaucratic process; does not necessarily lower incentive for hiring undocumented workers. |
| Foreign direct investment | Long-term strategy to reduce unauthorized immigration. | Short-term increase in migration possible. |
| Legalization or earned regularization | Identification of U.S. residents; legalizes a needed workforce. | Does not deter future illegal immigration and may encourage more. |
| Increase border enforcement | Could eventually lead to deterrence of unauthorized migration. | Cost of truly effective strategy could be exorbitant; marginal success to date; increased migrant deaths; possible increase in duration of stay; increased smuggling. |

In 1998 and 1999, the INS experimented with an alternative to raids, which it called Operation Vanguard. The idea was to use Social Security Administration (SSA) records to review employee eligibility in attempts to identify unauthorized workers without having to raid workplaces (*Rural Migration News*, 2001). The pilot project focused on meatpacking plants in the Midwest, where the INS subpoenaed employee records from more than 100 plants, compared their I-9 information against SSA records, identified workers who appeared to be unauthorized, and asked employers to resolve these discrepancies before official visits were made by INS agents. Although Operation Vanguard did not result in many deportations, it may have served as a deterrent to unauthorized immigration by reducing the desirability of meatpacking plants as places of employment for undocumented workers.

Operation Vanguard has been criticized by workers, farmers, and industry leaders for violating worker privacy rights and targeting Hispanics. Furthermore, the SSA stopped allowing the INS to check employee records against its databases in July 1999, citing privacy concerns and arguing that it can check worker status only if the INS has "reasonable cause" to believe that a worker is unauthorized (*Rural Migration News*, 2001). The governor of Nebraska established a commission to evaluate the effect of immigration enforcement; the commission recommended that Operation Vanguard not be resumed (*Rural Migration News*, 2001).

In March 1999, the INS announced a new interior enforcement strategy to "systematically combat illegal immigration inside the United States by attacking its causes, not merely its symptoms" (INS, 1999). The new strategy pledged to focus on criminal (rather than all illegal) immigrants, offered a stepped-up attack on smugglers and smuggling rings, and furthered the commitment to block and remove employers' access to undocumented workers without conducting raids (Uchitelle, 2000).

IIRIRA requires the INS to detain and deport foreigners who commit crimes that make them subject to deportation. This measure has been used more frequently in recent years: In 1986, the INS removed 1,978 aliens for criminal violations (INS, 2000). By 2000, 71,028 of the 184,775 aliens removed were criminals (INS, 2000). There have been a number of challenges to the strategy. Opponents argue that the policy went too far and that people were being detained for crimes they committed many years ago (*Migration News*, 1997). IIRIRA requires the INS to detain immigrants until their deportation. Especially problematic was the indefinite detention of "filters" or "nonremovable" criminal immigrants convicted in the United States whose country of origin refused to accept their return. A panel of five federal judges found these detentions to be excessive punishment and ordered the release of a number of immigrants (*Migration News*, March 1999). Opponents also point to cases of people who come to the United States as children and are later deported to countries they no longer recognize as their own. They also called attention to cases in which people were deported for minor infractions. For instance, crimes of "moral turpitude" were extended to include any crime that could draw a one-year sentence (*Migration News*, August 1999).

The new strategy also included a measure known as expedited removals, sanctioned by a provision of the IIRIRA, which allows immigration officers to remove at their discretion immigrants who lack proper documentation or use fraudulent documents. This provision has severely limited immigrants' rights to seek review by an immigration judge. Furthermore, the INS officer's determination, which is not subject to review, bars those removed from returning to the United States for five years and can lead to incarceration (Musalo et al., 2000).

First implemented on April 1, 1997, expedited removal procedures accounted for 46 percent of all removals in 2000 (INS, 2000). As the use of this measure has increased, immigrants rights groups and the American Civil Liberties Union have expressed concern over issues of due process.

## Reducing Employers' Incentives

Illegal immigration can also be reduced through labor market mechanisms, such as enforcing labor laws or imposing sanctions on those who hire illegal immigrants. Other industrialized nations rely heavily on this strategy to control illegal immigration, but it is rarely used in the United States (Cornelius, 1997).

In the United States, no level of government spends substantial resources to enforce labor and safety standards. As Cornelius (1997) notes:

> In the entire state of California, on an average day in 1994, only sixteen State Labor Commission inspectors were working to enforce the laws pertaining to payment of minimum wages and overtime, coverage by workers' compensation, tax withholdings by employers, environmental and other health and safety standards, in tens of thousands of businesses. Los Angeles County has only three such inspectors; San Diego County, one; and Orange County, none.

Furthermore, the resources allocated for enforcing labor and occupational standards have been declining over time (Cornelius, 1997). The U.S. Department of Labor had 19 percent fewer inspectors in 1996 than it had in 1986—fewer than 800 for the whole nation.

The enforcement of employer sanctions has also been limited. As noted earlier in this report, most employers are not penalized for hiring undocumented workers as long as they can prove that they examined the workers' papers and filed an I-9 form (Calavita, 1994). Employers are not required to verify the validity of the documents. Since the passage of IRCA, only a few fines have been levied on violators, and the amounts of the fines have been small (Fix and Hill, 1990; Cornelius, 2001; Peterson, 2001). For the policy to be effective, the INS would have to either employ a large number of inspectors or impose very high fees on employers.

Another option is to target industries that hire a large proportion of illegal immigrants. The fact that immigrants work in many industries, however, makes such targeting difficult. As Cornelius (1997) states:

> In the five U.S. states where an estimated 80 percent of all illegal immigrants now work (California, New York, Texas, Florida and Illinois), it is difficult to find a single industry of any economic consequence in which illegal immigrant labor is not amply represented, at some level. (p. 407)

Enforcement may be concentrated in a few industries (such as agriculture) that rely heavily on unauthorized workers, but these industries are not the major employers of illegal immigrants (Cornelius, 1997).

Finally, employer sanctions are politically unpopular. Both business and unions oppose them. Unions argue that sanctions further marginalize workers, drive down wages, and erode working conditions for immigrant workers in the United States (Bacon, 2001; Massey, Durand, and Malone, 2002). They have been able to block any changes that would make employers accountable for the people they hire (Calavitas, 1994; Cornelius, 1997). Although there seemed to be momentum in Congress to impose sanctions on businesses in the mid 1990s, the 1996 legislation approved only three pilot projects in five states, and employer participation was made voluntary (Cornelius, 1997).

## National Identification Card or System

Verifying an individual's legal presence and right to work in the United States could be achieved via a national identification card or system of identification cards. Under this proposal, every resident of the United States would be required to have an identification card with biometric data that could be scanned and tied to a central registry. Persons could be required to present such identification when applying for jobs or entering and exiting the United States.

In 1994, the U.S. Commission on Immigration Reform suggested the development of a system in which employers would call an automated phone-in system—similar to the system that is now used to obtain authorization for credit card purchases—to verify authorization for employment. The commission argued that fraud could be detected when a Social Security number is being used often or in many locations. However, the system depends on employers' compliance and on the quality of the INS verification systems (Zimmerman, 1991).[3]

Another proposal calls for the use of Social Security cards as identification cards. However, the Commissioner of Social Security, in testimony to Congress, estimated that it could cost between $3 billion

---

[3]IRCA included a fortification of existing verification systems and mandated the national adoption of the Systematic Alien Verification for Entitlement (SAVE) program. This program required state agencies administering federally funded benefits to verify the immigrant status of all noncitizens applying for services. The program has generated concerns about cost effectiveness and privacy issues, and problems with the quality of the data have also been found (Zimmerman, 1991).

and $6 billion and take more than 10 years to develop a more-secure Social Security card (Cornelius, 1997). Moreover, the SSA has argued in the past that the Social Security card should be used only for its present purpose.

Other suggestions have included using a system of identification cards in which Social Security cards, green cards, visas, and passports could all contain biometric data and be linked to a central registry. Such a system would not require the development of a new national identification card and would instead rely on preexisting sources of identification. A voluntary national identification card is yet another option. Those who elect to have such a card could use it to expedite travel and to establish identity for employment and other purposes. Individuals who elect not to obtain the card would be subject to lengthier inspections and identity checks.

Civil libertarians and others have cited privacy issues in their opposition to such proposals. Unions and immigrant advocates argue that employment cards criminalize workers, further marginalizing an already vulnerable population. Employment cards alone would not stop the flow of immigrants into the country or prevent unscrupulous employers from hiring or exploiting them (Bacon, 2001; Massey, Durand, and Malone, 2002). Implementation would also be daunting and extremely costly. Even in the aftermath of the September 11 attacks, President Bush indicated that he does not support a national identification card.

## Guest-Worker Programs

In 1917, the United States first allowed the recruitment of foreign workers, when the U.S. Department of Labor suspended the head tax and the literacy requirements for Mexican workers coming to work for U.S. farmers for a year (Martin, 1998). Since then, U.S. businesses have employed temporary workers from many parts of the world to work in agriculture, mining, railroad construction, and other labor-intensive industries. A formal guest-worker initiative, the Bracero Program, began in 1942, when domestic labor was scarce. It was the first and only time the United States engaged in a bilateral agreement to recruit workers. The Mexican government, sensitive to the exploitation of Mexican nationals, required the U.S. government to guarantee free housing, cooking facilities or meals provided at cost by employers, compensation insurance to cover expenses if the worker was injured at work, and round-trip transportation costs for workers. The first Bracero Program included provisions for minimum-wage pay or better and guaranteed Braceros payment for three-fourths of the period of time the farmer promised them work (Martin, 1998). No Mexican workers could be supplied to U.S. employers until the Department of Labor certified a shortage of Americans who were "able, willing, and qualified" to perform the work (Martin, 1998). The hope was that the program would prevent the hiring of illegal workers and that Mexicans would have less incentive to cross illegally. However, more immigrants came illegally during the first 10 years of the program than before, largely because employers preferred to hire illegal crossers rather than go through the bureaucratic process (García y Griego, 1998).

Soon after the program was established, discussions of employer sanctions began. Congress never approved these sanctions, and President Truman reluctantly signed an extension of the program in 1951 (Martin, 1998). Instead, in 1952, under pressure from the Mexican government, the U.S. Congress passed a law that made it illegal to "harbor, transport, or conceal illegal immigrants," as an attempt to impose some accountability on employers (Calavita, 1994). But an amendment to the law, the Texas proviso, excluded employment from the definition of harboring (Calavita, 1994). Two years later, political pressure against a growing unauthorized population in the United States led to the launch of "Operation Wetback" (Calavita, 1992). And the United States and Mexico sealed an agreement that eliminated many of the labor guarantees (García y Griego, 1998). Growers were able to hire as many Braceros as they deemed necessary, and illegal immigration virtually disappeared (García y Griego, 1998; Calavita, 1994). By the end of the Bracero Program in 1964, almost 5 million Mexican workers had been brought to the United States as Braceros, and almost that many had been apprehended in the United States (Lopez, 1981).

Since the termination of the Bracero Program in 1965, there have been periodic discussions about establishing other guest-worker programs. Farm owners, high-technology businesses, and the health-care industry regularly express the need for immigrant labor. In fact, some programs already exist for recruiting temporary workers. In 1986, the Special Agricultural Workers (SAW) Program was added to IRCA to recruit agricultural workers, but most SAWs no longer work in that field (Martin, 2002). H-1B and H-2A visas bring skilled and unskilled temporary workers to the United States, but employers insist that the programs are too complicated, have too many requirements, and do not bring in enough workers fast enough to meet labor demand (GAO, 1997b).

Recent proposals would establish new guest-worker programs for agriculture and other industries. One such proposed program would not tie workers to one employer and would allow the immigrant to "build equity" by participating in the program over time. Eventually, workers could readjust their status to establish permanent residence in the United States (Cornelius, 1997; Shimada, 1994). However, monitoring employers and employees in such a program could be daunting. The experience from the Bracero Program suggests that another guest-worker program *by itself* would not eliminate the incentives for hiring undocumented workers (Cornelius, 1997; García y Griego, 1983; Massey and Liang, 1989; Calavita, 1992). However, advocates maintain that a guest-worker program like the one proposed would formalize the migration that is currently taking place and would be preferable to the more furtive and unstable system in place now. A successful guest-worker program should include employer sanctions, enforce labor standards, and reduce the attractiveness of cheaper, undocumented labor to ensure that workers are not marginalized.

## Foreign Direct Investment

Another set of policy proposals focuses on improving labor market conditions in Mexico. The lack of economic opportunities in Mexico is the primary reason immigrants come to the United States. With the support of the United States, the Mexican government could improve these opportunities by continuing trade expansion and investing more heavily in infrastructure development, education, business development, and poverty-reduction programs.

NAFTA is, in part, a development strategy that includes built-in mechanisms for price and wage equalization that might eventually reduce migration (Martin, 2000). However, NAFTA and changes in the Mexican government's agricultural policies initially led to the displacement of many farmers and to increases in immigration (Martin, 2000; Cornelius 1997). Agriculture in Mexico became more large-scale and mechanized, and the prices of agricultural products dropped at the same time that the price of seeds and fertilizers increased, making it increasingly difficult for small farmers to make a living (Cornelius, 1997; Cornelius and Martin, 1993; Martin, 1993). Trade and economic growth in Mexico can reduce migration if accompanied by employment growth, improved labor standards, access to education, and increased equity. Otherwise, development and trade may lead to further displacement and outmigration (Cornelius and Martin, 1993).

Direct foreign investment on the part of the United States for infrastructure, education, business development, and poverty-reduction measures in Mexico would not be a quick fix for the illegal-immigration problem. The process of development could take generations (U.S. Commission for the Study of International Migration and Cooperative Economic Development, 1990; CONAPO, 2000). Furthermore, development might not diminish migration substantially in the traditional sending regions, where outmigration has become a way of life (Massey et al., 1987). The social networks developed by migrants in the United States over several generations strengthen the "culture of outmigration" in these regions and render border controls "increasingly useless" (Cornelius, 1997; Massey and Espinosa, 1997). However, potential migrants in new sending regions and perhaps younger adults in traditional sending regions might prefer to remain in Mexico if salaries and economic opportunities allowed them to make a decent living. In Cornelius's study of Mexican labor-exporting communities, residents demonstrated a strong desire for permanent, nonagricultural employment opportunities in their home communities (Cornelius, 1991). The study also suggested that the creation of such opportunities might be the *only* strategy that could significantly reduce unauthorized migration from these areas.

# Legalization or Regularization

Legalization, the granting of legal permanent residency to unauthorized residents of the United States, is one policy option that addresses the large number of unauthorized workers residing in the United States. Such a policy would bring a large portion of the unauthorized population to the surface, but a pure legalization program like IRCA seems unlikely. Although IRCA provided legal status to large numbers of unauthorized workers, it failed to meet its other primary objective: preventing future unauthorized immigration. Indeed, by creating a large pool of new permanent residents in the United States, IRCA almost certainly led to an increase in unauthorized immigration, as friends and family members living abroad came to join persons granted legalization in the United States. President Bush and many legislators have indicated they would not support outright legalization. However, incremental legalization is a possibility.

Recent bilateral talks between the United States and Mexico regarding immigration reform have included discussions of a new legalization program. One possible solution to the large number of unauthorized workers living in the United States lies in the creation of a "midpoint" status between temporary and permanent residence, with potential for incremental gains in status (*Migration News*, August 2001). Such an "earned legalization" program would encourage unauthorized Mexican workers who are currently living, working, and paying taxes in the United States to come forward, accept a temporary status, and accumulate "points" toward full permanent resident status (Senate Judiciary Committee Hearings, 2001). Thus far, the specific rules of an earned access system have not been clearly outlined.

# Summary

Crafting a successful immigration policy requires balancing a multitude of complex tradeoffs. This report does not advocate the adoption of a specific set of policies but rather presents some current alternatives for identifying unauthorized immigrants and regulating their flow.

No single policy can address all facets of unauthorized immigration. For example, a guest-worker program could solve employers' concerns regarding the supply of labor but would not by itself substantially reduce unauthorized immigration. A national identification card or employment verification card could reduce unauthorized immigration if it prevented unauthorized immigrants from finding jobs, but it would not address employers' labor needs or protect against labor abuses. Furthermore, political and economic pressures force policymakers into compromises that do not solve the problem. Even when potentially effective controls have been approved, as when employer sanctions were included in IRCA, they have been implemented in a way that made them ineffective. Ultimately, as the U.S. and Mexican economies become more interconnected, as long as economic opportunities in Mexico continue to be limited and a large wage difference between the two sides of the border persists, it will be difficult to deter those seeking a better standard of living for themselves and their families.

# Appendix A

# Data Sources

We conducted five focus groups and a community survey to gain qualitative understanding of the factors observed in our quantitative analysis. We also used a wide range of data sources from the United States and Mexico for our quantitative analyses. Mexican sources included:

- The *Encuesta Nacional sobre Migración en la Frontera Norte de México* (EMIF),
- The National Survey of Demographic Dynamics (ENADID) for 1992 and 1997, and
- The Mexican 2000 Census.

We also examined binational data, the MMP database, which includes survey data from more than 12,000 households in 71 communities in Mexico and more than 700 households in the United States.

Data sources in the United States included:

- The National Agricultural Statistics Service,
- The National Agricultural Workers Survey,
- The CPS from 1968 to 2000,
- California Employment Development Department data for employment in agriculture from 1983 to September 2001,
- The INS Southwest border apprehensions, border deaths, and legal entry data,
- Data from the California Rural Legal Assistance Foundation, and
- Data collected by the Center for Immigration Research, University of Houston, on deaths at the U.S.-Mexican border.

In this appendix, we present a description of the datasets used in our analysis, their limitations, and our restrictions. Descriptive statistics are given in Appendix B.

# Mexican Data Sources

## EMIF Data

The EMIF data are obtained through an annual survey of people temporarily located in 18 border-crossing Mexican communities along the U.S.-Mexican border. El Colegio de la Frontera Norte administered surveys to respondents in these border-crossing cities every year from 1993 to 1999. Face-to-face interviews with respondents captured the respondents' intention to migrate to the United States as well as information on previous migration and work experiences.

El Colegio de la Frontera Norte administers unique surveys to four distinct groups in the border cities: people migrating from southern Mexico, people migrating from northern Mexico (*la frontera norte*), people returning from the United States, and people who have been deported from the United States. For purposes of this report, we examined only data on migrants from the southern region.

The survey of people migrating from the southern region provides demographic information about each respondent, as well as prior work experience before migrating to the border city, reasons for not working if unemployed, and experiences during the trip to and within the border city. The survey asks about respondents' intentions for future migration in addition to information about their previous experiences of migration and employment in the United States. Respondents had to meet a set of criteria to be included in the survey: They had to be at least 13 years of age, not born in the United States, and nonresidents of the border city. Additionally, they had to have migrated to the border city to work, find work, visit family or friends, or conduct business, *with no specified date for return to their home city.* Beyond the requirements used by El Colegio de la Frontera Norte, we further restricted the sample to include only respondents who indicated plans to migrate to the United States within the next 30 days and/or respondents who had previous migration experience.

The result is a total sample for 1993–1999 of 9,680 who migrated from the southern region of Mexico to a border city and who intended to cross into the United States or had crossed previously. The breakdown of sample size by year is given in Table A.1.

Table A.1

Sample Sizes in the EMIF Data

| Year of Survey | Sample Size |
| --- | --- |
| 1993–1994 | 2,853 |
| 1994–1995 | 2,233 |
| 1996–1997 | 2,289 |
| 1998–1999 | 2,305 |

## INEGI Survey Data: 1992 and 1997 ENADID

In November 1992 and again in November 1997, the Mexican National Institute for Information and Geographic Statistics (INEGI) conducted an ENADID. Each of these surveys asked household heads to list the members of their households who had left the country to find work during the past five years. The survey collected personal information about each migrant, as well as place of departure, country of destination, and dates of departure and return for the most recent U.S. trip. In each of the ENADID surveys, migrants can be matched to their original households, permitting a direct comparison of those who migrated with those who did not. Furthermore, the surveys provide some information about the households from which the migrants came. The 1992 ENADID survey contained information for 7,412 international migrants; the 1997 survey had information for 8,160.

## INEGI Survey Data: Mexican 2000 Census

In February 2000, INEGI conducted surveys for the Mexican 2000 Census. As in the ENADID survey, one section asked for information on international migration among members of each household, including most of the questions asked during the previous ENADID surveys. The survey collected rudimentary demographic information about each migrant—age, gender, and place of departure—as well as the details of each migrant's most recent trip abroad.

The two ENADID surveys and the Mexican 2000 Census are nationally representative and include a large number of Mexican households. However, there is no way to match all migrants to the general files, which contain detailed information about each person in the sample. Hence, beyond age, gender, place of destination, and a few household variables (e.g., number of people in the household and type of flooring), we cannot capture anything about the immigrant or the household. The strength of the Mexican 2000 Census data, however, is its sample size: The migration file contains observations for 188,664 international migrants.

### Mexican Migration Project Database

Most of the modeling in this report is based on data from the MMP.[1] The data were collected in 71 Mexican communities between 1982 and 1998 (see Figure A.1). From two to five communities were surveyed in successive years, and a random sample of households was generated from each. The original MMP sample consisted of communities in the western part of Mexico, the major sending regions of immigrants to the United States (Durand, Massey, and Zenteno, 2000). As Mexican migration patterns have shifted (Marcelli and Cornelius, 2001), the MMP has collected data from communities that have become important sending regions in the 1990s (e.g., communities in Oaxaca, Veracruz, Puebla, and Baja California).

A sample frame of each community was constructed to draw a random sample of households for interviewing. In most small cities, towns, villages, and ranchos, the entire community was the sample frame, but to conserve resources, one working-class neighborhood was identified and sampled in cities with populations larger than 50,000.[2]

---

[1]For more on the sample, see Massey and Singer (1995); Lindstrom and Massey (1994).

[2]Durand's and Massey's rationale for conducting the survey is that only a very small percentage of the Mexican population lives abroad: In the 1930s, about 5.7 percent of Mexico's national population resided in the United States (García y Griego, 1989). In no other Census year between 1920 and 1980 has Mexico's immigrant population in the

SOURCE: MMP website.

**Figure A.1—Map of States Sampled by the MMP**

Two hundred households were interviewed in most communities, except in some ranchos, where 100 to 150 households were interviewed. Each head of household was questioned about all members of the household— everyone who lived in the house, whether or not they were relatives of the household head, and all children of the household head, whether or not they still lived in the sampled house.

The sample of permanent migrants in the United States was constructed from responses to the Mexican survey.[3] After gathering all the information on names and locations of possible contacts, interviewers were sent to interview people from the same Mexican communities who

---

United States exceeded 3 percent of Mexico's total population. Hence, selecting regions and counties where immigrants are known to reside reduces the cost of gathering information on international migrants.

[3]People were interviewed in the United States with the idea of including a sample of permanent settlers. It is possible that many of the immigrants with family in Mexico are temporary migrants. Hence, not including a sample of permanent settlers may underestimate the length of stay of immigrants and would overestimate the number of moves that end with migrants returning to Mexico.

were in the United States. Using snowball-sampling techniques, they gathered more information from these people about possible respondents in the United States. A snowball sample is also known as a reputational sample; it differs from random samples in that it relies on the personal contacts, friends, and family of the people interviewed to gather information about other prospective respondents (Goodman, 1961). In most cases, 20 outmigrant households were sampled; in smaller Mexican communities, 10 to 15 households were sampled.

The MMP interviewed 12,322 households. For most, the household head was the primary informant for the whole household. The study's questionnaire follows the logic of an ethnosurvey, blending qualitative and quantitative techniques. A semistructured interview required that specific information be gathered from each subject, but the actual wording and ordering of the questions was left to the judgment of the interviewer. This approach affords flexibility, but the quality of the information elicited depends strongly on the ability of the interviewer to gather information.[4]

In addition to gathering demographic data (age, education, marital status, number of children, and so on) and socioeconomic information (occupation, wages, and other economic variables) about all members of the household, the interviewer asked which people in the household had ever been to or were then in the United States. For those with migration experience, the interviewer recorded information about the first and most recent U.S. trips, including the year, duration, destination, U.S. occupation, legal status, hourly wage, and the total number of U.S. trips.

The interviews resulted in a total sample of 83,527 people, 15,645 of whom had lived in the United States at some point in their lives. The majority of the sample (85 percent) is constructed from those interviewed in Mexico; 15 percent were those interviewed in the United States as part of the snowball sample. Some respondents migrated to the United States more than once and are thus counted more than once in modeling the choice to return to Mexico. The number of times each

---

[4]Some researchers argue that because open questions do not force the respondent to an a priori way of looking at the world and a specified group of alternatives, they paint a better picture of the respondents' views and choices. For more on this, see Shuman and Presser (1981).

immigrant migrated is included in the database. However, the database includes information on the characteristics of the migrants for only the first and most recent migrations. For this reason, this study modeled the choice to remain in the United States or return to Mexico, based on the first and most recent immigration experiences.[5]

Although no other database provides a sample of households in both the United States and Mexico extensive enough to permit a comprehensive analysis of return migration, the MMP sample has limitations. The first problem is that the sample is not representative of the immigrant population in the United States.[6] It is, however, a representative sample of the relevant communities in the major sending regions in Mexico, and Mexico is the largest contributor of immigrants to California and the United States. The second problem is that the U.S. subsample is not a representative sample of the immigrant population from western Mexico. For this study, we approximated a representative sample by weighting.

Third, the snowball-sampling techniques used in the United States may systematically undersample people with little connection to the origin location or people living in nontraditional locations in the United States. For example, educated immigrants and those who obtain citizenship may be especially difficult to track using snowball sampling because they are more likely to have moved out of ethnic neighborhoods and may rely less heavily than other immigrants on ethnic connections.[7]

Fourth, collecting information about all members of the household from the head of the household may produce less-accurate information

---

[5]Using data on only the first and last migrations is not without problems, especially when dealing with a population in which permanent settlement may be a process that includes cyclical migration. However, 80 percent of the migrants who have been in the United States move either once or twice. Hence, although we include most of the trips, the results in this report underestimate the percentage of moves that result in return migration.

[6]A few tests have been done of the representativeness of the sample; for the most part, researchers find that the data source is consistent with the national sample. However, it oversamples migrant sending towns and therefore has more international migration than do national samples. For example, see Durand, Massey, and Zenteno (2000).

[7]See Saenz (1991); Bartel (1989).

about individuals. However, it would be impossible to generate relevant information about the characteristics and migration experience of those who no longer live in the household unless they happened to be visiting at the time of the interview. Measurement error in the independent variable will lead to downward bias in the estimates of the coefficients on moves.

Finally, the fact that we use retrospective rather than longitudinal data for U.S. immigrants creates a number of problems, including telescoping, which occurs when the respondent attributes an event to the incorrect time period. Forward telescoping occurs when the respondent includes events from a previous time period in the period being asked about. Backward telescoping occurs when the respondent pushes events backward to a period prior to the one being asked about. Both forward and backward telescoping may occur within the same interview. However, studies show that forward telescoping is more common, resulting in a net overreporting in most surveys.[8]

Retrospective data, unlike longitudinal data, may be more accurate at representing recent events than events from the past. For example, people may be very precise at estimating their current wages but may inflate or deflate the wages they earned 20 years ago. This will lead to a downward bias in the estimates.

Immigrants may also lie about their immigration status. However, since most of the immigrants are surveyed in Mexico and connections are built in the home community before people in the United States are interviewed, we trust that there would be little incentive to lie about immigration status.

Despite its drawbacks, the MMP dataset provides the most comprehensive sample of families in both Mexico and the United States for studying return migration. Most studies on Mexican immigrants either rely on U.S. Census data, which are limited to people living in the United States at one moment in time, or use survey data from one or two communities in Mexico. The Census cannot capture people who were in the United States at one time but are now living in Mexico, and the

---

[8]For more on telescoping and other sources of error, consult Sudman and Bradburn (1982).

community samples cannot capture the people who are now living in the United States. Furthermore, the limited community samples cannot capture differences among communities. Generalizing from the findings in one or two communities to the rest of the country may misrepresent migration patterns for all other communities.

The number and diversity of the communities in this sample, the number of people sampled in both Mexico and the United States, the breadth of information collected from individuals, families, and communities, and the retrospective nature of the survey allow for a comprehensive analysis of migration flows in and out of the country. Although the MMP sample is still a selected sample of communities in Mexico rather than a national sample, these communities are the major sending areas of Mexican immigrants to the United States.

# U.S. Data Sources

## National Agricultural Statistics Service Survey

The NASS collects data from a sample of farm operators four times per year. NASS sampling procedures are designed to ensure that farms of different sizes and new farms are included in the survey. The survey includes numerous questions on farms and farm operations, including the number of hired workers and wages paid to those workers. California is considered a separate region. According to the NASS:

> The relative sampling error for the number of hired workers generally ranged between 10 and 20 percent at the regional level. The U.S. all hired farm worker wage rate had a relative sampling error of 0.8 percent. The relative sampling error was 0.7 percent for the combined field and livestock worker wage rate. Relative sampling errors for the all hired farm worker wage rate generally ranged between 2 and 5 percent at the regional levels. (NASS, August 2001)

Because the NASS is a survey of farm operators rather than farm workers, it does not contain any detailed socioeconomic or demographic information on farm workers.

## National Agricultural Workers Survey

The NAWS is an annual random survey of farm workers. Sample sizes are around 2,500 per year. The survey is conducted three times per year in different seasons. The NAWS contacts workers at work sites, arranging for interviews to be conducted later. Agricultural employers are chosen randomly from public agency records. Detailed economic and demographic data are collected from the workers, including work authorization (legal status) and country of origin.

## INS Border Patrol—Border Death Data

Prior to FY 1999, the procedures for tracking and reporting migrant deaths were determined by individual Border Patrol sectors. No comparisons can be made prior to FY 1999 because of variations in reporting. In that fiscal year, the Border Patrol began keeping track of migrant deaths in accordance with guidelines issued by the INS, which instructed that bodies found by or reported to Border Patrol agents were to be documented and entered into a database specifically created to track migrant deaths.

Border Patrol data on migrant deaths are limited in several ways. First, the Border Patrol reports only deaths that occur along the U.S. side of the Southwest border. Bodies found in Mexico are not included. Second, the data cannot account for all migrant deaths within the United States. Many bodies go undiscovered or unreported and therefore are not included in the official count. Thus, the actual number of migrant deaths is higher than that shown in the Border Patrol data. Migrants who died in one fiscal year but were not found until the next year are included in the statistics for the fiscal year in which they were found.

## California Rural Legal Assistance Foundation

The Mexican Ministry of Foreign Relations provides the California Rural Legal Assistance Foundation with data on migrant deaths along the Southwest border. These data, which were originally collected by the Mexican consulates and the Mexican Foreign Ministry (SRE), have one important advantage over INS Border Patrol data: They include deaths of Mexican nationals who die on both sides of the border. Statistics for non-Mexican migrant deaths are collected informally by the Mexican consulates and are available for California only.

## Center for Immigration Research, University of Houston

The CIR reports probable migrant deaths using the vital registration system of the United States for 1984–1998. These data are limited to foreign-born nonresidents of the United States who die from external accidents and injuries in U.S. counties on and near the Southwest border.

The authors of the CIR report stress that the deceased are probably undocumented migrants, but vital registration data do not include immigration status or activity prior to death. Researchers have excluded causes of death that would have no relation to undocumented crossings (for example, suicides, drug overdoses, and airplane crashes). The remaining possible causes of death are highly linked to undocumented crossings: drownings, car–pedestrian accidents, hyperthermia, and hypothermia. Like the Border Patrol data, these data are limited to deaths that occur on the U.S. side of the border.

# Qualitative Data

As part of our study of Mexican migration and border enforcement, we conducted focus groups with unauthorized immigrants in California, as well as taking a survey of 184 households in a migrant-sending community in the state of Michoacan. Ideally, this sample of interviews supplements the quantitative analysis presented in previous chapters and gives us an opportunity to hear the migrants speak for themselves about their experiences. However, the sample is not a representative one that can be used to generalize about the experience of all unauthorized immigrants.

## Focus Groups

We conducted five focus groups in California—one in Fresno, one in Madera, and three in Los Angeles. A total of 52 immigrants participated—21 women and 31 men. The focus groups, which lasted about one hour, were conducted on May 25, June 29, and June 30, 2000.[9]

---

[9]We are indebted to Victoria Robinson for coordinating all the focus groups for us. Her help was invaluable.

The respondents were selected to include a mix of migrants in terms of year of migration, migration experience, occupations, regions in Mexico, countries of origin, and gender. In Los Angeles, two groups consisted only of men and another only of women; the other groups were of mixed gender. We collected data in Fresno and Madera to have a sample of recent immigrants working in agriculture. They were primarily Oaxaqueños, because we wanted a sample from a new sending region, believing that migration networks in such regions may not be as developed as those from more traditional sending regions in Mexico. We visited Los Angeles because it is the most important destination of Mexican unauthorized immigrants. We visited three worker sites—the West Los Angeles Day Labor Center, the Hollywood Job Center, and the United Domestic Workers site in Los Angeles. This last site afforded us valuable insights into the experience of women migrants in particular.

Because we were interested in interviewing an underground population, we relied on community contacts to arrange our interviews. These contacts helped us target the population and created confidence among the respondents. Jeffrey T. Ponting of California Rural Legal Assistance graciously helped us coordinate with the Frente Indigena Oaxaqueño Binacional (FIOB) to conduct interviews in Fresno and Madera. Rufino Domingues and Oralia Maceda from FIOB helped us find participants in the immigrant farm worker communities of Fresno and Madera. In Los Angeles, we relied on Abel Valenzuela, who had conducted a survey of day labor sites in Los Angeles for a forthcoming book. He put us in touch with representatives from the West Los Angeles Day Labor Center, the Hollywood Job Center, and the United Domestic Workers site in Los Angeles.

The average education of the respondents in this sample was low— only 5.5 years of education—and the average age was 31.6 years. Sixty-five percent of the respondents were single, but the majority (56 percent) had children. Seventy-three percent were originally from Mexico, and almost all were employed in low-skill occupations, as nannies, domestics, gardeners, waiters, painters, farm workers, or laborers in construction-related jobs. Most of the immigrants knew someone who was living in the United States at the time of their migration, and most of them received help arranging employment, housing, or transportation. Sixty percent of them were on their first trip, and more than half entered the United States after 1994. Ninety-three percent were unauthorized immigrants, and 89 percent used a smuggler to come across the U.S.-Mexican border. Finally, 60 percent plan to return to their country of origin.

The focus groups were conducted in Spanish, and where needed, a translator was available to translate from Spanish to Mixteco. The groups focused on the following topics:

- Reasons for coming to the United States,
- Plans to stay in the United States,
- Difficulty in crossing the border as compared with previous moves,
- Responses to the border enforcement build-up,
- Knowledge of the enforcement build-up before migration, and
- Opinions about the border policy and other policy options.

A short questionnaire was given to respondents at the end of the focus group discussion in order to gather some demographic data about the sample.

## Community Survey

In addition to convening the focus groups, we visited the town of Chavinda in the Mexican state of Michoacan to gather information about migrants and prospective migrants in the origin location.[10] For two weeks in January 2001, we conducted interviews of 184 households.

Chavinda is a small town in a predominantly agricultural area. It has a long history of sending migrants to the United States and, as such, is typical of other sending towns in the primary sending region of Mexico. Chavinda is an attractive town, with most of the homes well kept (including many vacant houses). Migrant dollars are an important source of income and prosperity in the town.

---

[10]We are indebted to Rafael Alarcón for helping us coordinate the survey in Chavinda and for providing us with access to his data collected in 1982 in the same community.

Using a list of households from a survey conducted in Chavinda in 1982 by Rafael Alarcón, we tried to visit the same families to observe changes in migration since 1982. Of the 184 housing units surveyed in 1982, 20 percent were vacant because the entire family had moved to the United States; another 10 percent were vacant, but the neighbors did not know the whereabouts of the original inhabitants (see Figure A.2).

There were 1,218 persons in the Chavinda sample in 1982 (see Table A.2). Of those, we were able to establish the location of 1,077 (88 percent). In 2001, 60 percent were in the United States—54 percent of those who were in Mexico in 1982 and 83 percent of those who were in the United States in 1982. This tremendous outmigration provides us with a rich set of data, albeit for one small town, in which to examine the timing of migration and attitudes toward increased border enforcement. In Chavinda, we used a survey similar to the 1982 original, although we added sections on migration history and knowledge of increased border enforcement. Some questions in the survey were open-ended, soliciting

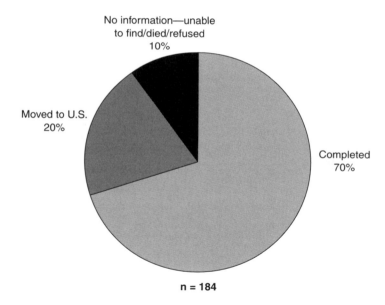

**Figure A.2—Reinterview Status of 1982 Sample in 2001**

Table A.2

Characteristics of the Chavinda Sample

| Residence Status | Number | Percentage |
|---|---|---|
| Resident of Chavinda in 1982 | 1,055 | |
| Known residence in 2001 | 925 | |
| Chavinda | 420 | 45 |
| Other Mexico | 7 | 1 |
| United States | 498 | 54 |
| Resident of United States in 1982 | 163 | |
| Known residence in 2001 | 152 | |
| Michoacan | 23 | 15 |
| Other Mexico | 3 | 2 |
| United States | 126 | 83 |

the respondent's opinions on the border policy and U.S. immigration policies, while others were more quantitative in nature.

Interviewers were sent to each home to ask for the people in the 1982 household. If the head of the 1982 household was available, interviewers used him or her for the second wave. If that person was not available but another adult in the 1982 household was available, the other adult served as the new informant. If no one in the 1982 household was accessible, an adult in the new household was asked to provide information about the people in the previous household and the new household. In only 10 percent of the cases could no information be gathered about the 1982 household (see Figure A.2).

The survey consisted of seven parts. In the first part, interviewers gathered information about the 1982 household (e.g., current place of residence, age, education, and occupation). Section 2 asked the same set of question of new members of the household. In Section 3, the interviewers asked about the migration of all family members, both those in the original sample and the new household members (e.g., number of trips since 1982, year of most recent trip, use of smugglers, legal status). The next section asked about family resources. For instance, people were asked if the family owned a telephone, a car, a satellite dish, land, or a business; whether they had running water; and whether they received any money from the United States. They were also asked about their perceptions of employment opportunities in Mexico and the United States. Section 6 asked the informant about his or her migration intentions as well as opinions on the border policy. The last section was for migrants only. If there was a migrant in the household and he or she was available, the interviewer asked detailed questions about every trip since 1982 and also asked for opinions about and knowledge of the build-up.

# Appendix B

# Empirical Analysis

Different statistical techniques were used to generate the results discussed in this report. In addition to descriptive statistics, we generated estimates of the immigrant population in the United States in Chapters 4 and 5. In Chapters 2 and 3, we used logistic regressions and discrete-time-hazard models to determine whether there was a change in the probability of migration over time; if a change was observed, we used these models to determine which factors could have led to the change. This appendix discusses the methods used in Chapters 2 and 3.

### Chapter 2: Changes in the Probability of Migration

- Logistic regression using the Mexican 2000 Census, 1992 ENADID, and 1997 ENADID to model the probability of migration 24 months prior to the survey year.
- Hierarchical discrete-time-hazard model using the MMP sample to model the probability of migration in 1970–1998.

### Chapter 3: Changes in the Duration of Stay in the United States

- Hierarchical discrete-time-hazard model using the MMP sample of the probability of return from the United States in 1970–1998 (measured for every year in the United States until return or until censored).
- Discrete-time-hazard model using Mexican 2000 Census, 1992 ENADID, and 1997 ENADID data on the probability of return for those who moved 24 months prior to the survey year (measured for every month in the United States prior to return or until censored).

## Logistic Regression: Probability of Migration

We used three nationally representative samples from Mexico—the 2000 Census, the 1992 ENADID, and the 1997 ENADID—to determine changes in the probability of migration in the 1990s. This allowed us to look at migration probabilities for two years prior to the enforcement build-up at the U.S.-Mexican border (from November 1990 to November 1992) and four years after the enforcement build-up (from November 1995 to November 1997 and from February 1998 to February 2000). We ran logistic regressions to model the probability of migration 24 months prior to the survey year.[1] In this model, an underlying response variable $Y_i$ is defined by the relationship

$$Y_i = \beta_0 + \beta_1 X_i + \beta_2 N_i + \beta_3 C_i + \beta_4 Y_i + \varepsilon_i, \tag{1}$$

where $X_i$ are individual characteristics of individual $i$, $N_i$ are family resources, $C_i$ are community characteristics, and $Y_i$ is a set of year dummies for the survey year. (The variables used in the model are described in Table B.1.) $\beta_0, \beta_1, \ldots, \beta_4$ are the coefficients to be estimated, and $\varepsilon_i$ is the error term. We assume that $\varepsilon_i$ follows a logistic distribution. Hence, the probability of migration is given by

$$\text{Prob } (Y_i = 1) = \frac{\exp(\beta_0 + \beta_1 X_i + \beta_2 N_i + \beta_3 C_i + \beta_4 Y_i)}{1 + \exp(\beta_0 + \beta_1 X_i + \beta_2 N_i + \beta_3 C_i + \beta_4 Y_i)}. \tag{2}$$

Our dataset consists of 120,680 migrants meeting all our criteria: 3,426 from 1992; 4,298 from 1997; and 112,956 from the more comprehensive Mexican 2000 Census. We used weighted regressions to account for the uneven distribution of observations across years.

## Hierarchical Discrete-Time-Hazard Model

Data restrictions limited the type of analysis we could do with the INEGI data.[2] To do a more detailed analysis of changes in trends, we had to rely on the MMP data. We estimated a set hierarchical discrete-

---

[1] We tried a number of other specifications, including the probability of migration within the last 12 months, the probability of migration within the last 24 months, and the probability of migration within the last five years. The trend did not change appreciably across models, and we chose to present this model.

[2] We know only if the person went to the United States in the last five years and some details about his or her last migration. The only personal characteristics we know are age and sex, and only three years of data are available.

## Table B.1

### Variable Definitions for Migration Model Using INEGI Data

| Variable | Description |
|---|---|
| Personal characteristics | |
| Age | Age at time of survey |
| Sex | Sex |
| Family resources | |
| Material of floor | Whether the house has dirt floors |
| Household members | Total number of household members |
| Community characteristics | |
| Size of community | If a small, large, or medium community |
| Mexican state | Dummies for the Mexican states |
| Year of survey | Dummies for 1992, 1997, or 2000 (1992 is left out) |

time-hazard models to observe changes in the probability of migration, remigration, and return from 1970 to 1998. This model allows us to determine the changes in the probability of migration and in the time it takes people to make a move.

In this model, as in the logistic model, there is an underlying response variable $Y_{it}$ defined by the relationship

$$Y_{it} = \beta_0 + \beta_1 X_{it} + \beta_2 N_{it} + \beta_3 C_{it} + \beta_4 M_{it} + \beta_5 T_i + \delta_1 Y_i + \varepsilon_{it}, \qquad (3)$$

where $X_{it}$ are the characteristics of individual $i$ on year $t$, $N_{it}$ are family resources and experiences at year $t$, $C_{it}$ are the characteristics of the community of origin at year $t$, $M_{it}$ are the individual's migration experience at year $t$, and $Y_i$ is the year at $t$. (The variables in these models are described in Table B.2.) $T_i$ is a set of dummy variables for duration of stay.[3] $\beta_0, \beta_1, \ldots, \beta_5,$ and $\delta_1$ are the coefficients to be estimated, and

---

[3]This vector varies depending on the decision model. In the first-migration model, $T$ is the years between 16 and 35 years of age. Hence it captures the time it takes to make a first trip to the United States. For the remigration model, $T$ is the number of years the person has been in Mexico since returning from his or her first trip to the United States. It then measures duration of stay in Mexico before a second move. For the return migration model, $T$ captures the number of years the immigrant has been in the United States, in order to measure how long it takes for an immigrant to return.

# Definition of the Variables Used in the Two-Stage Model of the Probability of First Migration, Remigration, and Return

| Variable | Description | Model |
|---|---|---|
| **Dependent variables** | | |
| Migration | = 1 if the person moved to the U.S. as an unauthorized immigrant at year $t$; otherwise is 0 | M |
| Remigration | = 1 if the person moved illegally to the U.S. at $t$; otherwise is 0 | RM |
| Return | = 1 if the person returned to Mexico at $t$; otherwise is 0 | R |
| **Duration variables** | | |
| Sixteen…twenty3 | Dummy variables for ages 16 to 23; this variable captures how long it takes to make a first trip to the U.S. (24 years old or older are left out). | M |
| Year1…Year5+ | Dummy variables for the number of years in Mexico since returning from the U.S. (more than five years in Mexico are left out). | RM |
| Year1…Year5+ | Dummy variables for the number of years in the U.S. (more than five years in the U.S. are left out). | R |
| **Personal characteristics** | | |
| age | age at year $t$ | RM,R |
| edyrsi | educational attainment at year $t$ | M,RM,R |
| head | = 1 if the person is a household head; otherwise is 0 | M,RM,R |
| **Household resources** | | |
| land | = 1 if the family owns land at year $t$; otherwise is 0 | M,RM,R |
| ownhome | = 1 if the family owns its home at year $t$; otherwise is 0 | M,RM,R |
| inusbft | = 1 if some family member is currently in the U.S. or has been in the U.S. in the last 10 years; otherwise is 0 | M,RM,R |
| legal | = 1 if someone in the family was legalized before $t$; otherwise is 0 | M,RM,R |
| **Community characteristics** | | |
| meninag | The proportion of men in the community of origin who work in agriculture | M,RM,R |
| small | If the population in the community of origin was less than 5,000 people at year $t$ (left out category) | M,RM,R |
| medium | If the population in the community of origin was between 5,000 and 50,000 people at year $t$ | M,RM,R |
| large | If the population of the community of origin was greater than 50,000 at year $t$ | M,RM,R |
| Michoacan | = 1 if from state of Michoacan; otherwise is 0 (left out category) | M,RM,R |
| Guanajuato | = 1 if from state of Guanajuato; otherwise is 0 | M,RM,R |
| Nayarit | = 1 if from state of Nayarit; otherwise is 0 | M,RM,R |

# Table B.2 (continued)

| Variable | Description | Model |
|---|---|---|
| Jalisco | = 1 if from the state of Jalisco; otherwise is 0 | M,RM,R |
| Zacatecas | = 1 if from the state of Zacatecas; otherwise is 0 | M,RM,R |
| Guerrero | = 1 if from the state of Guerrero; otherwise is 0 | M,RM,R |
| San Luis Potosi | = 1 if from the state of San Luis Potosi; otherwise is 0 | M,RM,R |
| Colima | = 1 if from the state of Colima; otherwise is 0 | M,RM,R |
| Oaxaca | = 1 if from the state of Oaxaca; otherwise is 0 | M,RM,R |
| Sinaloa | = 1 if from the state of Sinaloa; otherwise is 0 | M,RM,R |
| Baja California | = 1 if from the state of Baja California; otherwise is 0 | M,RM,R |
| Puebla | = 1 if from the state of Puebla; otherwise is 0 | M,RM,R |
| Aguas Calientes | = 1 if from the state of Aguas Calientes; otherwise is 0 | M,RM,R |
| Migration experience | | |
| agriculture | = 1 if working in agriculture while in the U.S.; otherwise is 0 (left out category) | RM,R |
| skilled | = 1 if skilled worker while in the U.S.; otherwise is 0 | RM,R |
| unskilled | = 1 if unskilled worker while in the U.S.; otherwise is 0 | RM,R |
| unemployed | = 1 if unemployed while in the U.S.; otherwise is 0 | RM,R |
| Los Angeles | = 1 if lived in Los Angeles while in the U.S.; otherwise is 0 (left out category) | |
| Other_CA | = 1 if lived in California but not Los Angeles while in the U.S.; otherwise is 0 | RM,R |
| Texas | = 1 if lived in Texas while in the U.S. the first time; otherwise is 0 | RM,R |
| Illinois | = 1 if lived in Illinois while in the U.S. the first time; otherwise is 0 | RM,R |
| Other_state | = 1 if lived in other parts of the nation while in the U.S. the first time; otherwise is 0 | RM,R |
| trips | Number of trips made to the U.S. | R |
| Year | | |
| yr1970...yr1998 | Dummy variables for years between 1970 and 1998 (1989 left out) | M,RM, R |
| Macro variables for second-stage model | | |
| Mexican GDP per capita | The GDP per capita for a particular year | M,RM, R |
| Exchange rate | Official exchange rate, pesos per dollar | M,RM, R |
| U.S. unemploy-ment rate | Annual unemployment rate in the U.S. | M,RM, R |
| Legal admissions | Total number of legal admission to the U.S. in a particular year | M,RM, R |
| Line watch hours | Total number of man-hours spent by the INS guarding the U.S.-Mexican border | M,RM, R |

$\varepsilon_i$ is the error term. We assume that $\varepsilon_i$ follows a logistic distribution. Hence, the probability of migration is given by

$$\text{Prob}(Y_{it} = 1) = \frac{\exp(\beta_0 + \beta_1 X_{it} + \beta_2 N_{it} + \beta_3 C_{it} + \beta_4 M_{it} + \beta_5 Y_i + \delta_1 T_i)}{1 + \exp(\beta_0 + \beta_1 X_{it} + \beta_2 N_{it} + \beta_3 C_{it} + \beta_4 M_{it} + \beta_5 Y_i + \delta_1 T_i)}$$

(4)

and it is specified for each year that an individual was observed (every record is a person-year).[4] The extended sample consisted of 329,515 person-years for the migration model and 17,871 for the remigration model.

The dependent variable is then the probability that person $i$ will migrate, given that $t$ years have elapsed. This model allows us to estimate the probability of migration over time better than a simple logistic equation does, while maintaining the simplicity of discrete models. It also allows us to observe the effects of the independent variables over time by having the independent variables interact with duration, which we did in some cases.

For these models, we selected people from communities surveyed after 1990 and looked only at the years since 1970. We also restricted the sample to respondents between 16 and 35 years of age to determine the probability of moving before age 35. In another model, we further restricted the sample to communities surveyed after 1994 to examine outmigration from new sending regions.

Given our data, we had two issues to address. First, some of the data were available at the person level, while other data varied only over time and were fixed for each person. Second, we had heteroskedasticity due to the smaller number of observations available to estimate the year dummies in the later years.

To correct the hierarchical structure of our data, we estimated a two-stage model. The first stage uses the person data to estimate the discrete-time-hazard model explained above. This stage explores whether

---

[4]Because we restricted the sample to persons between 16 and 35 years of age, the number of records available for each respondent equals either the number of years before migration or the number of years before censoring at age 35. $Y_{it} = 1$ if the person migrated in that particular year; otherwise $Y_{it} = 0$.

temporal changes in the characteristics of the sample or the communities of origin could have led to a change in the probability of migration. Next, a second-stage OLS regression takes the estimated coefficients for $\delta_1$ in stage 1 and attempts to control for macroeconomic conditions and the level of border enforcement to explain the time trend, as shown below:

$$\delta_1 = \alpha_0 + \alpha_1 MX_t + \alpha_2 US_t + \alpha_3 L_t + \alpha_4 B_t + \mu_t, \qquad (5)$$

where $MX_t$ are the economic conditions in Mexico in year $t$; $US_t$ are the conditions of the U.S. economy in year $t$; $L_t$ are the number of people admitted as legal permanent residents in year $t$, which captures the effect of IRCA on migration probabilities; and $B_t$ is the number of man-hours spent guarding the U.S.-Mexican border in year $t$, used to capture the effect of increased enforcement on migration behavior. Not doing this estimation in two stages would have affected the estimates of the standard error for the macro variables and may have led us to erroneously reject the null hypothesis that the variable has no effect on the time trend.

We address the issue of heteroskedasticity by weighting every observation in the second-stage OLS equation by 1/sqr *(n)*, where *n* is the number of observations available for each year. The later years are more imprecise because of smaller sample sizes, so this weighting should correct for the variance in the standard errors.

It bears emphasizing that a positive value for the dependent variable *returned, migration,* or *remigration* is not a permanent state. It indicates a change in residence in a particular year. Some of the migrants are engaging in cyclical migration and make many trips between Mexico and the United States. These models measure changes in location one trip at a time. Also, in the return migration model, return means that the migrant left the United States to return to Mexico, rather than necessarily having returned to his or her city of origin. This is also not necessarily a permanent move. People may have engaged in many more U.S. migrations after one trip to the United States.

# Discrete-Time-Hazard Model: Probability of Return

In addition to these models, we used the INEGI data to run a simple discrete-time-hazard model of the probability of return, with a restricted number of variables. The model includes only adults older than 15 who, at the time of the survey, claimed to have migrated for the last time to the United States two years prior to the survey year. The unit of analysis for this dataset is the migrant-month—that is, for each migrant, the dataset contains one observation for each month that he or she is in the United States. We then ran a simple discrete-time-hazard model to corroborate the trend found on the MMP sample using the INEGI data. Our dataset consists of 120,680 migrants meeting all our criteria: 3,426 from 1992; 4,298 from 1997; and 112,956 from the more comprehensive Mexican 2000 Census. When expanded to its final migrant-month form, the dataset contains 1,223,922 observations: 31,456 from 1992; 42,417 from 1997; and 1,150,049 from 2000.[5]

## Descriptive Statistics for All Models

In the following, we present the mean values for all the variables in the INEGI files for the migration and return models and the descriptive statistics of the MMP data for the return, remigration, and migration model.

### INEGI Data

As explained above, we used the INEGI data to estimate a simple logistic equation of the probability of migration and a discrete-time-hazard model of the probability of return. These samples are representative of the Mexican population in 1992, 1997, and 2000. They comprise people living in Mexico and family members who are considered part of the household and who migrated to the United States in the two years prior to the survey year, whether or not they are currently living in Mexico. The migration model uses the whole sample,

---

[5]Separate sets of regressions were estimated for men and women for each survey year and for all survey years together. Those for the combined model are shown below. Weights were included in the regressions.

and the return model uses only people who moved 24 months prior to the survey years.

As seen in Table B.3, only 1.6 percent of the Mexican population moved to the United States in the two years prior to the survey years. And 27 percent of those who moved within the 24 months prior to the survey years had already returned to Mexico by the time of the survey. The average age of the whole sample was 36; 48 percent were males; 15 percent of the people lived in a household with dirt floors; and 25 percent of the people lived in small towns in Mexico. The population was spread throughout the country, with 23 percent originating from the traditional sending states.[6] The average age in the INEGI migration samples was 29, substantially younger than the average age of the overall population, even after excluding people younger than 15. Seventy-nine percent of the migrants were males, and they were overrepresented among people living in small towns. They originated from a wide range of places in Mexico, but 52 percent of them were from the traditional sending states.

Table B.3

Descriptive Statistics of the INEGI Sample for the Migration and Return Models:  Men and Women 15 Years of Age and Older

| Variable | Overall Population | Migration File |
|---|---|---|
| Migration | 0.016 | |
| Return | | 0.266 |
| Age | 35.657 | 29.159 |
| Men | 0.484 | 0.789 |
| Dirt floors | 0.147 | 0.134 |
| Concrete floors | 0.541 | 0.612 |
| Household size | 5.254 | 4.987 |
| Small town | 0.247 | 0.434 |
| Large town | 0.496 | 0.262 |
| Aguas Calientes | 0.009 | 0.016 |
| Baja Norte | 0.024 | 0.016 |
| Baja Sur | 0.004 | 0.000918 |
| Campeche | 0.006 | 0.000867 |

[6]The traditional sending states are Aguas Calientes, Colima, Durango, Guanajuato, Jalisco, Michoacan, Nayarit, San Luis Potosi, and Zacatecas.

| Variable | Overall Population | Migration File |
|---|---|---|
| Coahuila | 0.024 | 0.018 |
| Colima | 0.005 | 0.008 |
| Chiapas | 0.035 | 0.004 |
| Chihuahua | 0.031 | 0.034 |
| Distrito Federal | 0.101 | 0.028 |
| Durango | 0.015 | 0.040 |
| Guanajuato | 0.047 | 0.114 |
| Guerrero | 0.030 | 0.046 |
| Hidalgo | 0.022 | 0.030 |
| Jalisco | 0.065 | 0.112 |
| México | 0.130 | 0.062 |
| Morelos | 0.015 | 0.021 |
| Nayarit | 0.009 | 0.017 |
| Nuevo Leon | 0.041 | 0.027 |
| Oaxaca | 0.033 | 0.032 |
| Puebla | 0.049 | 0.035 |
| Queretaro | 0.013 | 0.019 |
| Quintana Roo | 0.007 | 0.001 |
| San Luis Potosi | 0.023 | 0.044 |
| Sinaloa | 0.026 | 0.021 |
| Sonora | 0.023 | 0.01 |
| Tabasco | 0.018 | 0.001 |
| Tamaulipas | 0.029 | 0.028 |
| Tlaxcala | 0.009 | 0.004 |
| Veracruz | 0.072 | 0.032 |
| Yucatán | 0.016 | 0.004 |
| Zacatecas | 0.014 | 0.046 |

## MMP Sample

As explained above, we looked at the information for persons older than 15 at the time of survey in communities interviewed after 1990. Then we looked at the years between ages 16 and 35 to determine the migration probabilities of these individuals. The sample for each model was slightly different. For the migration model, we looked at the whole sample of people, whether they had migrated to the United States or not. For the return model, we selected only the migrants and looked at the years they spent in the United States, independent of where they were living at the time of survey. Finally, for the remigration model, we selected the sample of people who moved once to the United States and returned to Mexico, so that we could determine their probability of remigration. This generates completely different samples, as shown in Table B.4.

## Table B.4

## Mean Values for the Variables Used in the Probability-of-Migration Models

| Variable | Migration | Remigration | Return |
|---|---|---|---|
| yr1970 | 0.022 | 0.004 | 0.006 |
| yr1971 | 0.024 | 0.006 | 0.008 |
| yr1972 | 0.025 | 0.007 | 0.01 |
| yr1973 | 0.026 | 0.01 | 0.01 |
| yr1974 | 0.028 | 0.012 | 0.016 |
| yr1975 | 0.029 | 0.016 | 0.019 |
| yr1976 | 0.031 | 0.019 | 0.023 |
| yr1977 | 0.032 | 0.022 | 0.025 |
| yr1978 | 0.034 | 0.027 | 0.031 |
| yr1979 | 0.036 | 0.032 | 0.036 |
| yr1980 | 0.037 | 0.038 | 0.04 |
| yr1981 | 0.039 | 0.042 | 0.04 |
| yr1982 | 0.04 | 0.046 | 0.04 |
| yr1983 | 0.042 | 0.044 | 0.039 |
| yr1984 | 0.043 | 0.048 | 0.043 |
| yr1985 | 0.045 | 0.053 | 0.049 |
| yr1986 | 0.046 | 0.057 | 0.054 |
| yr1987 | 0.048 | 0.063 | 0.055 |
| yr1988 | 0.049 | 0.072 | 0.059 |
| yr1990 | 0.051 | 0.059 | 0.057 |
| yr1991 | 0.046 | 0.052 | 0.055 |
| yr1992 | 0.039 | 0.045 | 0.045 |
| yr1993 | 0.034 | 0.037 | 0.041 |
| yr1994 | 0.032 | 0.038 | 0.044 |
| yr1995 | 0.025 | 0.033 | 0.036 |
| yr1996 | 0.02 | 0.023 | 0.026 |
| yr1997 | 0.016 | 0.02 | 0.02 |
| yr1998 | 0.01 | 0.013 | 0.012 |
| age | 24.32 | 25.8 | 24.72 |
| years of education | 8.11 | 6.6 | 7.0 |
| head | 0.197 | 0.345 | 0.199 |

Table B.4 (continued)

| Variable | Migration | Remigration | Return |
|---|---|---|---|
| land | 0.208 | 0.221 | 0.255 |
| own home | 0.586 | 0.612 | 0.631 |
| in U.S. before | 0.338 | 0.541 | 0.732 |
| legal | 0.113 | 0.158 | 0.251 |
| male ag worker | 0.421 | 0.466 | 0.452 |
| medium-size town | 0.415 | 0.48 | 0.429 |
| large town | 0.246 | 0.115 | 0.104 |
| Guanajuato | 0.121 | 0.141 | 0.123 |
| Jalisco | 0.094 | 0.175 | 0.152 |
| Michoacan | 0.078 | 0.135 | 0.103 |
| Nayarit | 0.036 | 0.049 | 0.039 |
| Zacatecas | 0.14 | 0.158 | 0.18 |
| Guerrero | 0.06 | 0.03 | 0.06 |
| San Luis Potosi | 0.153 | 0.11 | 0.141 |
| Colima | 0.046 | 0.051 | 0.057 |
| Oaxaca | 0.06 | 0.028 | 0.029 |
| Sinaloa | 0.057 | 0.051 | 0.039 |
| Puebla | 0.06 | 0.016 | 0.019 |
| Baja California | 0.06 | 0.024 | 0.026 |
| Aguas Calientes | 0.035 | 0.033 | 0.035 |
| agriculture | | 0.301 | 0.195 |
| skilled | | 0.131 | 0.188 |
| unskilled | | 0.42 | 0.485 |
| unemployed | | 0.142 | 0.133 |
| Trips | | | 3.9 |
| Los Angeles | | 0.328 | 0.354 |
| Other_CA | | 0.357 | 0.326 |
| Texas | | 0.141 | 0.095 |
| Illinois | | 0.046 | 0.08 |
| Other_state | | 0.128 | 0.145 |
| Expanded sample | 499,466 | 40,381 | 17,871 |

SOURCE: MMP.

Compared with the overall population, migrants are older, a greater proportion of them are household heads, more own land or a home, more originate from households with other migrants, and more have other family members who have been legalized to live in the United States. Also, a greater proportion of them originated from towns with a large proportion of males employed in agriculture, and a greater proportion originated from Guanajuato, Jalisco, or Michoacan. Of the migrants, those who returned to Mexico after their first trips were even older and had less education than the sample of all migrants. They were even more likely to have originated from an agricultural town in one of the major sending states, and they were more likely to be a household head. Compared with the sample of all migrants, they were also more likely to have worked in agriculture in the United States and to have lived in Texas.

# Empirical Results

In this section we present the results of all the models. The tables present the odd ratios for some of the coefficients in the models and their respective standard errors.

## Migration and Remigration Models

In Chapter 2 we used the MMP data to run two models, one to determine the probability of making a first migration to the United States (Table B.5) and the other to determine the probability of making a second migration to the United States for those with previous migration experience (Table B.6). The tables show the results for the full model for both men and women.[7]

We also used the INEGI data to estimate a model of the probability of having moved to the United States in the two years prior to the survey year. The results are shown in Table B.7.

## Length of Stay in the United States

Next we present the results of the models in Chapter 3, where we estimated two different sets of models using two different data sources. The first set used the MMP data to estimate a detailed model of the probability of return (Table B.8). We then used the data collected by INEGI in 1992 and 1997 and the Mexican 2000 Census to estimate a discrete-time-hazard model of the probability of return (Table B.9).

---

[7]The results of the restricted model of communities surveyed after 1994 are available upon request from the authors.

## Table B.5

### Odds Ratios and Standard Errors for the Time-Hazard Model of the Probability of First Migration (MMP Data)

| Variable | Men | | Women | |
|---|---|---|---|---|
| | Odds Ratio | Standard Error | Odds Ratio | Standard Error |
| yr1970 | 0.51*** | 0.1238 | 0.47** | 0.2431 |
| yr1971 | 0.32*** | 0.1437 | 0.21*** | 0.3337 |
| yr1972 | 0.49*** | 0.1199 | 0.29*** | 0.2791 |
| yr1973 | 0.54*** | 0.1143 | 0.48** | 0.2195 |
| yr1974 | 0.51*** | 0.1141 | 0.71* | 0.185 |
| yr1975 | 0.68*** | 0.1027 | 0.61** | 0.1895 |
| yr1976 | 0.54*** | 0.1087 | 0.61** | 0.1834 |
| yr1977 | 0.57*** | 0.1047 | 0.63** | 0.1758 |
| yr1978 | 0.72*** | 0.0958 | 0.84 | 0.1557 |
| yr1979 | 0.72*** | 0.0944 | 0.62** | 0.1681 |
| yr1980 | 0.68*** | 0.0941 | 0.97 | 0.1429 |
| yr1981 | 0.41*** | 0.1093 | 0.30*** | 0.2083 |
| yr1982 | 0.53*** | 0.099 | 0.32*** | 0.2003 |
| yr1983 | 0.41*** | 0.1065 | 0.47*** | 0.171 |
| yr1984 | 0.70*** | 0.0901 | 0.57*** | 0.1571 |
| yr1985 | 0.73*** | 0.0884 | 0.69** | 0.1458 |
| yr1986 | 0.80** | 0.0858 | 0.60*** | 0.1491 |
| yr1987 | 0.67*** | 0.0898 | 0.59*** | 0.1483 |
| yr1988 | 0.89 | 0.0829 | 0.80* | 0.1341 |
| yr1990 | 0.97 | 0.0805 | 0.98 | 0.1244 |
| yr1991 | 0.78** | 0.0886 | 0.92 | 0.1318 |
| yr1992 | 0.77** | 0.0943 | 0.99 | 0.1376 |
| yr1993 | 0.78** | 0.0986 | 0.97 | 0.1431 |
| yr1994 | 0.86 | 0.0963 | 0.93 | 0.1453 |
| yr1995 | 0.97 | 0.1023 | 0.74* | 0.1737 |
| yr1996 | 0.95 | 0.1161 | 0.50** | 0.2347 |
| yr1997 | 0.76* | 0.1431 | 0.60** | 0.2509 |
| yr1998 | 0.54** | 0.2116 | 0.56* | 0.3195 |
| Age dummies | | | | |
| sixteen | 2.24*** | 0.0599 | 1.56*** | 0.1091 |
| seventeen | 2.89*** | 0.0552 | 2.04*** | 0.0985 |
| eighteen | 3.57*** | 0.0517 | 2.11*** | 0.0971 |
| nineteen | 3.08*** | 0.0545 | 2.43*** | 0.0923 |
| twenty | 3.05*** | 0.0546 | 2.88*** | 0.0867 |
| twenty1 | 2.26*** | 0.0609 | 2.02*** | 0.0995 |
| twenty2 | 2.09*** | 0.0629 | 2.19*** | 0.097 |
| twenty3 | 1.75*** | 0.068 | 1.95*** | 0.1021 |
| years of education | 1.16*** | 0.0153 | 1.22*** | 0.0288 |

| Variable | Men | | Women | |
|---|---|---|---|---|
| | Odds Ratio | Standard Error | Odds Ratio | Standard Error |
| years of education2 | 0.99*** | 0.001 | 0.99*** | 0.00183 |
| head | 1.58*** | 0.0411 | 2.78*** | 0.1552 |
| land | 0.98 | 0.0379 | 0.90* | 0.0615 |
| own home | 0.88*** | 0.035 | 0.81*** | 0.0538 |
| in U.S. before | 2.63*** | 0.037 | 6.87*** | 0.0684 |
| legal | 0.54*** | 0.0509 | 0.84** | 0.0651 |
| male ag worker | 1.81*** | 0.1285 | 1.24 | 0.2271 |
| medium-size town | 0.89** | 0.0371 | 0.82** | 0.0644 |
| large town | 0.60*** | 0.0863 | 0.76* | 0.146 |
| State dummies | Yes | | Yes | |
| Sample size | 242,391 | | 254,278 | |

NOTES: *** p ≤ 0.001   ** p ≤ 0.05   * p ≤ 0.10.

## Table B.6

### Odds Ratios and Standard Errors for the Time-Hazard Model of the Probability of Remigration (MMP Data)

| Variable | Men | | Women | |
|---|---|---|---|---|
| | Odds Ratio | Standard Error | Odds Ratio | Standard Error |
| yr1970 | 0.43 | 0.7426 | 2.60 | 1.134 |
| yr1971 | 0.55 | 0.5434 | 1.36 | 1.1367 |
| yr1972 | 0.99 | 0.408 | 0.99 | 1.1248 |
| yr1973 | 0.52 | 0.451 | 0.00 | 532 |
| yr1974 | 0.58 | 0.3807 | 0.42 | 1.0824 |
| yr1975 | 0.76 | 0.3212 | 0.33 | 1.0708 |
| yr1976 | 0.78 | 0.2941 | 0.26 | 1.0593 |
| yr1977 | 0.84 | 0.2828 | 0.90 | 0.6006 |
| yr1978 | 0.95 | 0.2563 | 0.88 | 0.5501 |
| yr1979 | 0.78 | 0.2491 | 0.31 | 0.7745 |
| yr1980 | 0.64* | 0.2477 | 0.62 | 0.5418 |
| yr1981 | 0.59** | 0.2466 | 0.76 | 0.4845 |
| yr1982 | 0.48** | 0.2549 | 0.20** | 0.7702 |
| yr1983 | 0.41** | 0.2752 | 0.42 | 0.5867 |
| yr1984 | 0.65* | 0.237 | 0.85 | 0.4633 |
| yr1985 | 0.80 | 0.2198 | 1.22 | 0.4047 |
| yr1986 | 0.88 | 0.2035 | 0.74 | 0.4263 |

| Variable | Men | | Women | |
|---|---|---|---|---|
| | Odds Ratio | Standard Error | Odds Ratio | Standard Error |
| yr1987 | 0.51** | 0.224 | 0.79 | 0.4041 |
| yr1988 | 0.86 | 0.1897 | 0.67 | 0.4125 |
| yr1990 | 1.02 | 0.1974 | 1.48 | 0.371 |
| yr1991 | 1.29 | 0.1982 | 1.38 | 0.3913 |
| yr1992 | 0.95 | 0.2255 | 0.60 | 0.5107 |
| yr1993 | 1.33 | 0.2252 | 1.47 | 0.4516 |
| yr1994 | 1.66** | 0.2123 | 3.19** | 0.3875 |
| yr1995 | 2.22*** | 0.2125 | 3.19** | 0.4004 |
| yr1996 | 1.30 | 0.2732 | 2.07 | 0.5415 |
| yr1997 | 2.91*** | 0.2455 | 3.68** | 0.5926 |
| yr1998 | 3.10*** | 0.3281 | 6.63** | 0.5841 |
| year 1 | 1.33** | 0.1108 | 1.55** | 0.2164 |
| year 2 | 2.66*** | 0.1036 | 2.31*** | 0.2217 |
| year 3 | 1.73*** | 0.1197 | 1.91** | 0.2465 |
| year 4 | 1.24 | 0.1424 | 1.07 | 0.3081 |
| age | 1.04 | 0.0769 | 1.16 | 0.1511 |
| age2 | 1.00 | 0.00148 | 1.00 | 0.00299 |
| years of education | 1.04 | 0.0366 | 0.97 | 0.0818 |
| years of education2 | 1.00* | 0.00242 | 1.00 | 0.00531 |
| head | 1.55*** | 0.1181 | 1.36 | 0.4282 |
| land | 0.90 | 0.0925 | 1.22 | 0.1847 |
| own home | 0.98 | 0.0877 | 0.92 | 0.1681 |
| in U.S. before | 2.10*** | 0.1097 | 2.41** | 0.2706 |
| legal | 0.98 | 0.1119 | 0.89 | 0.1666 |
| male ag worker | 0.75 | 0.307 | 0.52 | 0.6784 |
| medium-size town | 0.80** | 0.1012 | 0.88 | 0.2145 |
| large town | 0.52** | 0.218 | 1.24 | 0.4222 |
| State dummies | Yes | | Yes | |
| U.S. experience | Yes | | Yes | |
| Sample size | 13,153 | | 4,274 | |

NOTES: *** $p \leq 0.001$    ** $p \leq 0.05$    * $p \leq 0.10$.

## Table B.7

### Odds Ratios and Standard Errors for the Logistic Model of the Probability of Migration (INEGI Data)

| Variable | Odds Ratio | Standard Error |
|---|---|---|
| Intercept | 1.231 | 0.034 |
| Age | 0.980 | 0.000 |
| Age2 | 1.000 | 2.99E-06 |
| Sex | 2.051 | 0.000 |
| Dirt floors | 0.832 | 0.001 |
| Concrete floors | 1.096 | 0.000 |
| Household size | 1.129 | 0.000 |
| Small | 1.299 | 0.000 |
| Large | 0.674 | 0.000 |
| Yr97 | 1.040 | 0.000 |
| Yr00 | 0.922 | 0.000 |
| State dummies | yes | |

NOTE: All coefficients are statistically significant at a 5 percent level

## Table B.8

### Parameter Estimates and Standard Errors for the Time-Hazard Model of the Probability of Return (MMP Data)

| | Men | | Women | |
|---|---|---|---|---|
| | Odds Ratio | Standard Error | Odds Ratio | Standard Error |
| yr1970 | 0.60** | 0.1808 | 0.87 | 0.5854 |
| yr1971 | 0.71** | 0.1649 | 1.30 | 0.4038 |
| yr1972 | 0.57*** | 0.1594 | 0.35** | 0.51 |
| yr1973 | 0.67** | 0.1421 | 0.36** | 0.3935 |
| yr1974 | 0.61*** | 0.1375 | 0.58* | 0.2936 |
| yr1975 | 0.57*** | 0.1311 | 0.31*** | 0.315 |
| yr1976 | 0.75** | 0.1226 | 0.45** | 0.2727 |
| yr1977 | 0.65*** | 0.123 | 0.45** | 0.2561 |
| yr1978 | 0.58*** | 0.1184 | 0.44*** | 0.2384 |
| yr1979 | 0.68*** | 0.11 | 0.55** | 0.2157 |
| yr1980 | 0.74** | 0.1068 | 0.66** | 0.2006 |
| yr1981 | 0.67*** | 0.1091 | 0.64** | 0.1981 |
| yr1982 | 0.72** | 0.1095 | 0.70* | 0.2026 |
| yr1983 | 0.68*** | 0.1135 | 0.51** | 0.2281 |
| yr1984 | 0.69*** | 0.1103 | 0.69* | 0.2049 |
| yr1985 | 0.64*** | 0.1062 | 0.69* | 0.1955 |

| | Men | | Women | |
|---|---|---|---|---|
| | Odds Ratio | Standard Error | Odds Ratio | Standard Error |
| yr1986 | 0.87 | 0.0993 | 0.78 | 0.1885 |
| yr1987 | 0.88 | 0.0993 | 0.87 | 0.1809 |
| yr1988 | 1.54*** | 0.0933 | 0.96 | 0.1751 |
| yr1990 | 1.08 | 0.0992 | 0.83 | 0.1762 |
| yr1991 | 1.33** | 0.0998 | 1.01 | 0.173 |
| yr1992 | 1.30** | 0.1093 | 1.32 | 0.1767 |
| yr1993 | 0.70** | 0.1295 | 0.67* | 0.213 |
| yr1994 | 1.17 | 0.1137 | 0.74 | 0.2082 |
| yr1995 | 1.12 | 0.1224 | 0.85 | 0.2109 |
| yr1996 | 1.00 | 0.1361 | 0.62* | 0.2714 |
| yr1997 | 1.18 | 0.1423 | 1.01 | 0.2718 |
| yr1998 | 0.78 | 0.2114 | 1.40 | 0.3019 |
| year 1 | 1.78*** | 0.0555 | 1.24* | 0.1129 |
| year 2 | 7.27*** | 0.0521 | 4.45*** | 0.0928 |
| year 3 | 3.41*** | 0.0606 | 3.06*** | 0.1033 |
| year 4 | 2.24*** | 0.0715 | 1.96*** | 0.1227 |
| age | 1.23*** | 0.0325 | 1.15** | 0.0648 |
| age2 | 1.00*** | 0.000642 | 1.00** | 0.00128 |
| years of education | 0.98 | 0.0163 | 0.99 | 0.0328 |
| years of education2 | 1.00 | 0.00109 | 1.00 | 0.00213 |
| head | 1.80*** | 0.0464 | 1.70** | 0.1895 |
| land | 1.23*** | 0.0422 | 1.17** | 0.0807 |
| own home | 1.18*** | 0.04 | 0.96 | 0.0708 |
| in U.S. before | 0.62*** | 0.0424 | 0.69*** | 0.0968 |
| legal | 0.91** | 0.0489 | 1.01 | 0.0728 |
| male ag worker | 3.27*** | 0.1377 | 4.88*** | 0.2971 |
| medium-size town | 1.02 | 0.0438 | 1.12 | 0.0886 |
| large town | 1.66*** | 0.0977 | 1.85** | 0.1873 |
| State dummies | Yes | Yes | Yes | Yes |
| U.S. experience | Yes | Yes | Yes | Yes |
| Sample size | 27,865 | 10,773 | 11,146 | 4,605 |

NOTES: ***$p \leq 0.001$    ** $p \leq 0.05$    * $p \leq 0.10$.

## Table B.9

## Odds Ratios, Parameter Estimates, and Standard Errors for the
## Time-Hazard Model of the Probability of Return
## (INEGI Data)

| Variable | Odds Ratio | Parameter Estimate | Standard Error |
|---|---|---|---|
| Intercept | | −5.3078 | 0.0104 |
| Age | 1.078*** | 0.0751 | 0.000419 |
| Age2 | 0.999*** | −0.00064 | 5.23E-06 |
| Sex | 1.312*** | 0.2718 | 0.0033 |
| Dirt floors | 0.787*** | −0.2395 | 0.0045 |
| Concrete floors | 0.908*** | −0.097 | 0.00292 |
| Household size | 1.087*** | 0.083 | 0.000461 |
| Small | 0.999 | −0.00076 | 0.00299 |
| Large | 1.15*** | 0.1396 | 0.00339 |
| Yr97 | 0.689*** | −0.373 | 0.00262 |
| Yr00 | 0.318*** | −1.1453 | 0.00346 |
| mo0 | 0.32*** | −1.1388 | 0.00665 |
| mo1 | 0.54*** | −0.6159 | 0.00566 |
| mo2 | 0.67*** | −0.3998 | 0.00538 |
| mo3 | 0.807*** | −0.214 | 0.00518 |
| mo4 | 0.802*** | −0.2207 | 0.00524 |
| mo5 | 0.772*** | −0.2592 | 0.00534 |
| mo7 | 0.82*** | −0.1987 | 0.00537 |
| mo8 | 0.722*** | −0.3261 | 0.00562 |
| mo9 | 0.468*** | −0.7594 | 0.00648 |
| mo10 | 0.319*** | −1.1441 | 0.00746 |
| mo11 | 0.333*** | −1.1005 | 0.00736 |
| mo12 | 0.397*** | −0.9246 | 0.00693 |
| mo13 | 0.271*** | −1.3053 | 0.00802 |
| mo14 | 0.138*** | −1.9789 | 0.0106 |
| mo15 | 0.152*** | −1.8815 | 0.0102 |
| mo16 | 0.129*** | −2.0512 | 0.011 |
| mo17 | 0.117*** | −2.1443 | 0.0114 |
| mo18 | 0.116*** | −2.1559 | 0.0115 |
| mo19 | 0.064*** | −2.7419 | 0.015 |
| mo20 | 0.107*** | −2.2381 | 0.0119 |
| mo21 | 0.042*** | −3.1625 | 0.0183 |
| mo22 | 0.017*** | −4.0879 | 0.0286 |
| mo23 | 0.003*** | −5.8968 | 0.0699 |
| mo24 | 0.002*** | −6.2557 | 0.0834 |
| State dummies | Yes | | |

NOTES: ***p ≤ 0.001.

# References

Alarcon, R., *Immigrants or Transitional Workers? The Settlement Process Among Mexicans in Rural California,* The California Institute for Rural Studies, Davis, California, 1995a.

Alarcon, R.,"Transnational Communities, Regional Development, and the Future of Mexican Immigration," *Berkeley Planning Journal,* Vol. 10, 1995b, pp. 36–54.

Allen, Mike, and Bill Miller, "Bush Proposes Tracking System for Noncitizens," *Washington Post,* January 26, 2002, p. A11.

Andreas, Peter, *Border Games: Policing the U.S.-Mexico Divide*, Cornell University Press, Ithaca, New York, 2000.

Andreas, Peter, "The Transformation of Migrant Smuggling Across the U.S.-Mexico Border," in David Kyle and Rey Koslowski (eds.), *Global Human Smuggling: Comparative Perspectives,* The Johns Hopkins University Press, Baltimore, Maryland, 2001, pp. 108–125.

Associated Press, "Four Bodies Found in All-American Canal," March 24, 2000.

Associated Press, "Security Tightened on Great Lakes Travel to and from Canada," April 21, 2002.

Bacon, David, "Employer Sanctions—The Political Economy of Undocumented Immigration in the U.S.," *Sweatshop Watch*, May 2001.

Bartel, Ann, "Where Do the New U.S. Immigrants Live?" *Journal of Labor Economics,* Vol. 72, No. 4, 1989.

Bean, Frank D., Roland Chanove, Robert G. Cushing, Rodolfo de la Garza, Gary P. Freeman, Charles W. Haynes, and David Spener, *Illegal Mexican Migration and the United States/Mexico Border: The Effects of Operation Hold the Line on El Paso/Juarez,* U.S. Commission on Immigration Reform, Population Research Center, University of Texas at Austin, 1994, pp. 38–42.

Bean, Frank D., Rodolfo Corona, Rodolfo Tuirán, and Karen A. Woodrow-Lafield, "The Quantification of Migration Between Mexico and the United States," in *Migration Between Mexico and the United States, Binational Study*, Vol. 1, Mexican Ministry of Foreign Affairs and U.S. Commission on Immigration Reform, Mexico City and Washington, D.C., 1998, pp. 1–90.

Bean, Frank D., Rodolfo Corona, Rodolfo Tuirán, Karen A. Woodrow-Lafield, and Jennifer Van Hook, "Circular, Invisible, and Ambiguous Migrants: Components of Difference in Estimates of the Number of Unauthorized Mexican Migrants in the United States," *Demography*, Vol. 38, No. 3, 2001.

Bean, Frank D., Barry Edmonston, and Jeffrey S. Passel (eds.), *Undocumented Migration to the United States: IRCA and the Experience of the 1980s*, Urban Institute Press, Washington, D.C., 1990.

Bean, Frank D., Allan G. King, and Jeffrey S. Passel, "The Number of Illegal Migrants of Mexican Origin in the United States: Sex Ratio-Based Estimates for 1980," *Demography*, Vol. 20, 1983a, pp. 99–109.

Bean, Frank D., Allan G. King, and Jeffrey S. Passel, "Estimates of the Size of the Illegal Migrant Population of Mexican Origin in the United States: An Assessment, Review, and Proposal," in H. Browning and R. de la Garza (eds.), *Mexican Immigrants and Mexican Americans: An Evolving Relation*, CMAS Publications, University of Texas Press, Austin, Texas, 1983b, pp. 13–16.

Bean, Frank D., Jennifer Van Hook, and Karen Woodrow-Lafield, *Estimates of Numbers of Unauthorized Migrants Residing in the United States: The Total, Mexican, and Non-Mexican Central American Unauthorized Populations in Mid-2001*, Pew Hispanic Center, Washington, D.C., 2001.

Bean, Frank D., Georges Vernez, and C. B. Keely, *Opening and Closing the Doors: Evaluating Immigration Reform and Control*, Urban Institute Press, Washington, D.C., 1989.

Booth, William, "Emotions on the Edge; Arizona Ranchers Face Tide of Mexicans Along Border," *Washington Post*, June 21, 2000, p. A1.

Budget of the United States Government, Department of Justice, Washington, D.C., appendices, various years.

Calavita, Kitty, *Inside the State: The Bracero Program, Immigration and the INS,* Routledge, New York London, 1992.

Calavita, Kitty, "U.S. Immigration and Policy Responses: The Limits of Legislation," in Wayne Cornelius, Philip L. Martin, and James F. Hollifield (eds.), *Controlling Immigration: A Global Perspective,* Stanford University Press, Stanford, California, 1994, pp. 55–82.

Clark, Rebecca L., Jeffrey S. Passel, Wendy N. Zimmerman, and Michael E. Fix, *Fiscal Impacts of Undocumented Aliens: Selected Estimates for Seven States,* Urban Institute, Washington, D.C., 1994.

*Consejo Nacional de Población CONAPO, Migración México-Estados Unidos, Opciones de Política,* Rodolfo Tuirán, *Coordinador, Secretariá de Gobernación, la Secretariá de Relaciones Exteriores y El Consejo Nacional de Población,* 2000.

Cornelius, Wayne, *Mexican Migration to the United States: Causes, Consequences, and U.S. Responses,* Massachusetts Institute of Technology, Cambridge, Massachusetts, monograph, 1978, p. 10.

Cornelius, Wayne, *America in the Era of Limits: Nativist Reactions to the "New" Immigrants,* Center for U.S.-Mexico Studies, University of California San Diego, La Jolla, Research Report Series, No. 3, 1982.

Cornelius, Wayne, "Labor Migration to the United States," in Sergio Diaz-Briquets and Sidney Weintrab (eds.), *Regional and Sectoral Development in Mexico as Alternatives to Migration,* Westview Press, Boulder, Colorado, 1991.

Cornelius, Wayne, *Inside the State: The Bracero Program, Immigration and the INS,* Routledge, New York and London, 1992.

Cornelius, Wayne, "Appearance and Realities: Controlling Illegal Immigration in the United States," in Myron Weiner and Tadashi Hanami (eds.), *Temporary Workers or Future Citizens? Japanese and U.S. Immigration Policies,* New York University Press, New York, 1997, pp. 384–427.

Cornelius, Wayne, "The Structure Embeddedness of Demand for Mexican Immigrant Labor: New Evidence from California," in Marcelo Suarez-Orozco (ed.), *Crossings: Mexican Immigration in Interdisciplinary Perspective,* Harvard University Press/David Rockefeller Center for Latin American Studies, Cambridge, Massachusetts, 1998, pp. 114–144.

Cornelius, Wayne, "Death at the Border: Unintended Consequences of U.S. Immigration Control Policy," *Population and Development Review*, Vol. 27, No. 4, 2001, pp. 661–685.

Cornelius, Wayne, and Philip L. Martin, "The Uncertain Connection: Free Trade and Rural Mexican Migration to the United States," *International Migration Review*, Vol. 27, No. 3, 1993, pp. 484–512.

Cornelius, Wayne, Philip L. Martin, and James F. Hollifield (eds.), *Controlling Immigration: A Global Perspective,* Stanford University Press, Stanford, California, 1994.

Costanzo, Joe, Cynthia Davis, Caribert Irazi, Daniel Goodkind, and Roberto Ramirez, *Evaluating Components of International Migration: The Residual Foreign Born*, U.S. Census Bureau, Population Division Working Paper #61, 2002.

Crane, Keith, Beth J. Asch, Joanna Zorn Heilbrunn, and Danielle C. Cullinane, *The Effect of Employer Sanctions on the Flow of Undocumented Immigrants to the United States*, RAND, Santa Monica, California, 1990.

Cross, H. E., and J. A. Sandos, *Across the Border: Rural Development in Mexico and Recent Migration to the United States,* Institute of Governmental Studies, University of California, Berkeley, 1981.

Deardorff, Kevin E., and Lisa M. Blumerman, *Evaluating Components of International Migration: Estimates of the Foreign-Born Population by Migrant Status in 2000,* U.S. Census Bureau, Population Division Working Paper #58, 2001.

Delves Broughton, Philip, "Fox Models His Vision of North America on EU," *The Daily Telegraph*, August 10, 2001.

Donato, Katharine, "Changes in the Game of Cat-and-Mouse at the Border: The Consequences of Immigration Reform," paper presented at the Third Binational Conference on Mexico-U.S. Migration, Puerto Vallarta, Mexico, March 2002.

Donato, Katharine M., Jorge Durand, and Douglas S. Massey, "Stemming the Tide? Assessing the Deterrent Effect of the Immigration Reform and Control Act," *Demography*, Vol. 29, 1992, pp. 139–158.

Durand, Jorge, and Douglas S. Massey, "Mexican Migration to the United States: A Critical Review," *Latin American Research Review,* Vol. 27, No. 2, 1992, pp. 3–42.

Durand, Jorge, Douglas S. Massey, and Rene M. Zenteno, "Mexican Immigration to the United States: Continuities and Change," *Latin American Research Review,* 2000.

Eschbach, Karl, Jaqueline Hagan, and Nestor Rodriguez, "Causes and Trends in Migrant Deaths along the U.S.-Mexico Border, 1985– 1998," Center for Immigration Research, University of Houston, 2001.

Eschbach, Karl, Jaqueline Hagan, Nestor Rodriguez, Ruben Hernandez-Leon, and Stanley Bailey, "Death at the Border," *International Migration Review,* Vol. 33, No. 2, 1999, pp. 430–454.

Espenshade, Thomas J., "Undocumented Migration to the United States: Evidence from a Repeated Trials Model," in Frank D. Bean, Barry Edmonston, and Jeffrey S. Passel (eds.), *Undocumented Migration to the United States: IRCA and the Experience of the 1980s,* Urban Institute Press, Washington, D.C., 1990, pp. 159–181.

Espenshade, Thomas J., "Does the Threat of Border Apprehension Deter Undocumented U.S. Immigration?" *Population and Development Review,* Vol. 20, No. 4, 1994, pp. 871–892.

Espenshade, Thomas J., Jessica L. Baraka, and Gregory A. Huber, "Implications of the 1996 Immigration Reforms," *Population and Development Review,* Vol. 23, No. 4, 1997, pp. 769–801.

Fernandez, Edward W., and J. Gregory Robinson, "Illustrative Ranges of the Distribution of Undocumented Immigrants by State," Population Division, U.S. Bureau of the Census, Washington, D.C., unpublished paper, 1994.

Fix, Michael (ed.), *The Paper Curtain: Employer Sanctions' Implementation, Impact, and Reform,* Urban Institute Press, Washington, D.C., 1991.

Fix, Michael, and Paul T. Hill, *Enforcing Employer Sanctions: Challenges and Strategies,* Urban Institute Press, Washington, D.C., 1990.

Fix, Michael, and Jeffrey A. Passel, *Immigration and Immigrants: Setting the Record Straight,* Urban Institute, Washington, D.C., 1994.

Fox, Ben, "Volunteers Hope Water Stations Save Immigrants' Lives in Desert," Associated Press State and Local Wire, July 26, 2000.

García y Griego, Manuel, "The Importation of Mexican Contract Laborers to the United States, 1942–1964: Antecedents, Operation, and Legacy," in Peter G. Brown and Henry Shue (eds.), *Migrants and U.S. Responsibility,* Rowman & Litterfield, Totowa, New Jersey, 1983, pp. 49–98.

García y Griego, Manuel, "The Mexican Labor Supply, 1990–2010," in Wayne A. Cornelius and Jorge Bustamante (eds.), *Mexican Migration to the U.S.: Origins, Consequences and Policy Options,* University of California, San Diego, 1989.

García y Griego, Manuel, "The Bracero Program," in *Migration Between Mexico & the United States: Binational Study, Volume 3*, Research Report and Background Materials, Mexico-United States Binational Migration Study for the Mexican Ministry of Foreign Affairs and the U.S. Commission on Immigration Reform, 1998.

Gimpel, James, and James R. Edwards, Jr., *The Congressional Politics of Immigration Reform,* Allyn and Bacon, Needham Heights, Massachusetts, 1999.

Goodman, L., "Snowball Sampling," *Annals of Mathematical Statistics,* Vol. 32, 1961, pp. 117–151.

Gribbin, August, "U.S. Seeks Mutual 'Security Perimeter,'" *The Washington Times,* November 26, 2001, Part A, p. A4.

Hanson, Gordon, and Antonio Spilimbergo, "Political Economy, Sectoral Shocks, and Border Enforcement," NBER, Working Paper 7315, 1999.

Heyman, Josiah M., "Putting Power in the Anthropology of Bureaucracy: The Immigration and Naturalization Service at the Mexico-United States Border," *Current Anthropology*, Vol. 26, No. 2, 1995, pp. 261–287.

Higham, John, *Strangers in the Land: Patterns of American Nativism, 1860–1925,* Rutgers University Press, New Brunswick, New Jersey, 1955.

Ibarra, Ignacio, "180 Troops Called upon to Help Federal Agencies Guard Border," *Arizona Daily Star* (Tucson), February 21, 2002.

"Injured Mexican Immigrants Will File Suit Against Arizona Vigilantes." *La Voz de Aztlan,* May, 18, 2000.

Janofsky, Michael, "Immigrants Flood Border in Arizona, Angering Ranchers," *The New York Times,* June 18, 2000, p. A1.

Johnson, Hans P., *Undocumented Immigration to California: 1980–1993,* Public Policy Institute of California, San Francisco, California, 1996.

Johnson, Hans P., "Has Increased Border Enforcement Tightened U.S. Labor Markets?" Public Policy Institute of California, San Francisco, California, Working Paper, 2002.

Keely, Charles B., "Counting the Uncountable: Estimates of Undocumented Aliens in the United States," *Population and Development Review,* Vol. 3, No. 4, 1977, pp. 473–481.

Kennedy, Edward M., "U.S.-Mexico Migration Discussions: An Historic Opportunity," prepared testimony as Senator and Chair, Senate Judiciary Committee, Federal News Service, Inc., September 7, 2001.

Kirstein, Peter N., *Anglo over Bracero: A History of the Mexican Workers in the United States from Roosevelt to Nixon,* Saint Louis University, Ph.D. dissertation, 1973.

Kiser, George C., and Martha Woody Kiser (eds.), *Mexican Workers in the United States: Historical and Political Perspectives,* University of New Mexico Press, Albuquerque, New Mexico, pp. 120–121.

Kossoudji, Sherrie A., "Playing Cat and Mouse at the U.S.-Mexico Border," *Demography,* Vol. 29, No. 2, 1992, pp. 159–180.

Lellingwood, Ken, and Esther Schrader, "Ranchers on Border Raise Tensions over Immigrants," *Los Angeles Times,* May 17, 2000, p. A3.

Lindstrom, D. P., and D. S. Massey, "Selective Emigration, Cohort Quality, and Models of Immigrant Assimilation," *Social Science Research,* Vol. 23, 1994, pp. 315–349.

Lopez, Gerald P., "Undocumented Mexican Migration: In Search of a Just Immigration Law and Policy," *UCLA Law Review,* Vol. 28, April 1981, pp. 615–714.

Lowell, B. Lindsay, and Richard Fry, "Estimating the Distribution of Undocumented Workers in the Urban Labor Force: Technical

Memorandum to *How Many Undocumented: The Numbers Behind the U.S.-Mexico Migration Talks,* Pew Hispanic Center, Washington, D.C., 2002.

Lowell, B. Lindsay, and Roberto Suro, *How Many Undocumented: The Numbers Behind the U.S.-Mexico Migration Talks,* Pew Hispanic Center, Washington, D.C., 2002.

Marcelli, Enrico, and Wayne Cornelius, "The Changing Profile of Mexican Migrants to the United States: New Evidence from California and Mexico," *Latin American Research Review*, Vol. 36, No. 3, 2001, pp. 105–131.

Marquis, Christopher, "I.N.S. Proposes New Limits on the Length of Visas," *The New York Times,* April 9, 2002.

Martin, Philip, *Trade and Migration: NAFTA and Agriculture,* Institute for International Economics, Washington, D.C., 1993.

Martin, Philip, "Good Intentions Gone Awry: IRCA and U.S. Agriculture," *The Annals of American Academy,* Vol. 534, 1994, pp. 44–57.

Martin, Philip, "Mexican-U.S. Migration: Policies and Economic Impacts," *Challenge*, April 1995.

Martin, Philip, "The Endless Debate: Immigration and U.S. Agriculture," in Peter Duignan and Lewis Gann (eds.), *The Debate in the United States over Immigration,* Hoover Institution, Stanford, California, 1998, pp. 79–101. Available at http://www-hoover.stanford.edu/.

Martin, Philip, "Trade and Migration: The Mexico-U.S. Case," in Slobodan Djajic (ed.), *International Migration: Trends, Policy and Economic Impact,* Routledge, London, 2000.

Martin, Philip, *Guest Workers: New Solution, New Problem?* Pew Hispanic Center, Washington, D.C., 2002.

Massey, D. S., "Social Structure, Household Strategy, and the Cumulative Causation of Migration," *Population Index,* Vol. 56, 1990, pp. 3–26.

Massey, D. S., R. Alarcon, J. Durand, and H. Gonzalez, *Return to Aztlan: The Social Process of International Migration from Western*

*Mexico,* University of California Press, Berkeley and Los Angeles, 1987.

Massey, D. S., Jorge Durand, and Nolan J. Malone, *Beyond Smoke and Mirrors: Mexican Immigration in an Era of Economic Integration,* Russell Sage Foundation, New York, 2002.

Massey, D. S., and K. Espinosa, "What's Driving Mexico-U.S. Migration? A Theoretical, Empirical, and Policy Analysis," *American Journal of Sociology,* Vol. 102, No. 4, 1997, pp. 939–999.

Massey, D. S., and Audrey Singer, "New Estimates of Undocumented Mexican Migration and the Probability of Apprehension," *Demography,* Vol. 32, 1995, pp. 203–213.

Massey, Douglas, and Zai Liang, "The Long-Term Consequences of a Temporary Worker Program: The U.S. Bracero Experience," *Population Research and Policy Review,* Vol. 8, No. 3, 1989, pp. 199–226.

McCarthy, Kevin F., and Georges Vernez, *Immigration in a Changing Economy,* RAND, Santa Monica, California, 1997.

McDonnell, Patrick J., and Jonathan Peterson, "Skeptics Wary of Impending INS Split, Restructuring: Details Are Sketchy About How the Two New Bureaus Would Be Organized," *Los Angeles Times,* April 29, 2002.

Meissner, Doris, "A New Deal with Mexico," *Washington Post,* August 8, 2001.

*Migration News,* Vol. 4 , No. 11, November 1997. Available at http://migration.ucdavis.edu/mn/index.html.

*Migration News,* Vol. 6, No. 3, March 1999.

*Migration News,* Vol. 6, No. 8, August 1999.

*Migration News,* Vol. 7, No. 3, March 2000.

*Migration News,* Vol. 8, No. 7, July 2001.

*Migration News,* Vol. 8, No. 8, August 2001.

*Migration News,* Vol. 8, No. 10, October 2001.

Musalo, Karen, Lauren Gibson, Stephen Knight, and J. Edward Taylor, *The Expedited Removal Study: Report on the First Three Years of Implementation of Expedited Removal,* Center for Human Rights and

International Justice, University of California, Hastings College of the Law, San Francisco, 2000.

National Agricultural Statistics Service, *Fact Finders for Agriculture: Farm Labor*, August 1998a.

National Agricultural Statistics Service, *Fact Finders for Agriculture: Farm Labor*, November 1998b.

National Agricultural Statistics Service, *Fact Finders for Agriculture: Farm Labor*, February 2000a.

National Agricultural Statistics Service, *Fact Finders for Agriculture: Farm Labor*, August 2000b.

National Agricultural Statistics Service, *Fact Finders for Agriculture: Farm Labor*, August 2001.

National Research Council, *The New Americans: Economic, Demographic, and Fiscal Effects of Immigration*, James P. Smith and Barry Edmonston (eds.), National Academy Press, 1997.

Navarro, Mireya, "On California's Urban Border, Praise for Immigration Curbs," *The New York Times*, Section 1, August 21, 2001, p. 1.

Newman, Gerald L., "The Lost Century of American Immigration Law," *Columbia Law Review*, Vol. 93, No. 8, 1993, pp. 1833–1901.

Orrenius, Pia, "Illegal Immigration and the Southwest Border," *The Border Economic*, Federal Reserve Bank of Dallas, June 2001.

Orrenius, Pia, "The Role of U.S. Border Enforcement in the Crossing Behavior of Mexican Migrants," paper presented at the Third Binational Conference on Mexico-U.S. Migration, Puerto Vallarta, Mexico, March 2002.

Passel, Jeffrey S., "Undocumented Immigrants: How Many?" *Proceedings of the Social Statistics Section of the American Statistical Association Meeting*, Washington, D.C., 1985, pp. 65–72.

Passel, Jeffrey S., "Demographic Analysis: An Evaluation," *U.S. Census Monitoring Board, Final Report to Congress*, 2001a. Available at www.cmbp.gov.

Passel, Jeffrey S., *Some Random Thoughts on Undocumented Immigration, Census 2000, Demographic Analysis, A.C.E. and the CPS*, Urban Institute, Washington, D.C., 2001b.

Passel, Jeffrey S., and Michael F. Fix, *U.S. Immigration at the Beginning of the 21st Century,* Testimony Before the Subcommittee on Immigration and Claims Hearing on "The U.S. Population and Immigration," Committee on the Judiciary, U.S. House of Representatives, Urban Institute, Washington, D.C., 2001.

Passel, Jeffrey S., and K. A. Woodrow, "Change in the Undocumented Alien Population in the United States, 1979–1983," *International Migration Review,* Vol. 21, 1987, pp. 1304–1334.

Peterson, Jonathan, "INS Penalty System Falls Down on Job," *Los Angeles Times,* August 6, 2001.

Portes, Alexandro, and Richard Bach, *Latin Journey: Cuban and Mexican Immigrants in the United States,* Berkeley University Press, Berkeley, California, 1985.

Reisler, Mark, *By the Sweat of Their Brow: Mexican Immigrant Labor in the United States: 1900–1940,* Greenwood Press, Westport, Connecticut, 1976.

Reuters, "Complaints of Abuse at U.S.-Mexico Border Draw U.N. Envoy's Visit," *Chicago Tribune,* May 17, 2000, p. A16.

Reyes, Belinda I., "Immigrant Trip Duration: The Case of Immigrants from Western Mexico," *International Migration Review,* Vol. 35, 2001, pp. 1185–1204.

Rooney, Kevin D., Capitol Hill Hearing Testimony, House Judiciary Committee, Immigration and Claims Subcommittee, May 15, 2001.

Ruppe, David, "Fox Addresses Congress: Urges U.S. Government to Give Increased Trust, Cooperation," http://abcnews.com, September 6, 2001.

*Rural Migration News,* Vol. 7, No. 1, January 2001. Available at http://migration.ucdavis.edu/mn/index.html.

Saenz, Rogelio, "Interregional Migration Patterns of Chicanos: The Core, Periphery, and Frontier," *Social Science Quarterly,* Vol. 72, No. 1, March 1991.

Samora, Julian, *Los Mojados: The Wetback Story,* University of Notre Dame Press, Notre Dame, Indiana, 1971.

Sanchez, Lionel, "Top U.N. Rights Official Hears from Critics of Immigration Crackdown," *San Diego Union-Tribune,* November 27, 1999, Section B-12.

Sanchez, Lionel, "County Spent $50 Million on Immigrants in '99, Study Finds," *San Diego Union-Tribune*, February 6, 2001, Section B-1.

Shimada, Haruo, *Japan's "Guestworkers": Issues and Public Policies,* University of Tokyo Press, Tokyo, distributed by Columbia University Press, New York, 1994.

Shuman, Howard, and Stanley Presser, *Questions and Answers in Attitude Survey: Experiments on Question Form, Wording and Context,* Academic Press, New York, 1981.

Singer, Audrey, and Douglas S. Massey, "The Social Process of Undocumented Border Crossing Among Mexican Migrants," *International Migration Review*, 1998.

Smith, James F., and Ken Ellingwood, "September 11 Leaves Carpet Loomers Idle in Oaxacan Town," *Los Angeles Times*, November 28, 2001.

Spener, David, "Smuggling Migrants Through South Texas: Challenges Posed by Operation Rio Grande," in David Kyle and Rey Koslowski (eds.), *Global Human Smuggling: Comparative Perspectives,* The Johns Hopkins University Press, Baltimore, Maryland, 2001, pp. 115–137.

Sudman, Seymour, and Norman M. Bradburn, *Asking Questions: A Practical Guide to Questionnaire Design,* Jossey-Bass Publishers, San Francisco, California, 1982.

TheNewsMexico.com, "Record-Breaking Amount of Money Enters Mexico from U.S.," October 23, 2001.

Uchitelle, Louis, "INS Is Looking the Other Way as Illegal Immigrants Fill Jobs," *The New York Times*, March 9, 2000.

United States Commission for the Study of International Migration and Cooperative Economic Development, *Unauthorized Migration: An Economic Development Response,* Washington, D.C., 1990.

United States General Accounting Office, *INS' Southwest Border Strategy: Staffing and Enforcement Activities,* Washington, D.C., 1996.

United States General Accounting Office, *Illegal Immigration: Southwest Border Strategy Results Inconclusive; More Evaluation Needed,* report to the Committee on the Judiciary, U.S. Senate, and the Committee on the Judiciary, U.S. House of Representatives, Washington, D.C., 1997a.

United States General Accounting Office, *H-2a Agricultural Guest Worker Program: Changes Could Improve Services to Employers and Better Protect Workers,* report to the U.S. Congressional Committees, Washington, D.C., 1997b.

United States General Accounting Office, *U.S.-Mexico Border: Issues and Challenges Confronting the United States and Mexico,* report to the Committee on the Judiciary, U.S. Senate, and the Committee on the Judiciary, U.S. House of Representatives, Washington, D.C., 1999a.

United States General Accounting Office, *Illegal Immigration: Southwest Border Strategy Results Implementation,* report to the Committee on the Judiciary, U.S. Senate, and the Committee on the Judiciary, U.S. House of Representatives, Washington, D.C., 1999b.

United States General Accounting Office, *INS' Southwest Border Strategy: Resource and Impact Issues Remain After Seven Years,* Washington, D.C., 2001.

United States House of Representatives, Committee on the Judiciary, Oversight Hearing on Illegal Immigration Issues, 106th Cong., 2d Sess., June 10, 1999. Available at http://www.house.gov/judiciary/barn0611.htm.

United States Immigration and Naturalization Service, *Annual Report,* U.S. Department of Justice, Washington, D.C., 1978.

United States Immigration and Naturalization Service, *1995 Statistical Yearbook of the Immigration and Naturalization Service,* Washington, D.C., 1997a.

United States Immigration and Naturalization Service, *Cracking Down on Aliens Smuggling: Progress Report,* Washington, D.C., October 1997b.

United States Immigration and Naturalization Service, *Backgrounder: Interior Enforcement Strategy,* U.S. Department of Justice, Washington, D.C., March 29, 1999.

United States Immigration and Naturalization Service, *Statistical Yearbook of the Immigration and Naturalization Service,* Washington, D.C., 2000.

United States Immigration and Naturalization Service, *INS Factsheet: Border Patrol Recruiting and Hiring,* April 22, 2002.

United States/Mexico Border Counties Coalition, *Illegal Immigrants in U.S./Mexico Border Counties: The Costs of Law Enforcement, Criminal Justice, and Emergency Medical Services,* University of Arizona, Tucson, 2001, p. 252.

United States Senate Judiciary Committee Hearings, "U.S.-Mexico Migration Discussions: An Historic Opportunity," Federal News Service, Inc., September 7, 2001.

U.S.-Mexico Binational Commission (BMC), "Joint Press Availability: With Mexican Secretary of Foreign Relations Rosario Green," May 18, 2000, http://www.state.gov/www/regions/wha/000518_usmex_binational.html.

U.S.-Mexico Migration Panel, *Mexico-U.S. Migration: A Shared Responsibility,* Carnegie Endowment for International Peace and the Instituto Tecnologico Autonomo de Mexico, 2001.

Van Hook, Jennifer, and Frank Bean, "Estimating Unauthorized Mexican Migration to the United States: Issues and Results," in *Migration Between Mexico and the United States, Binational Study*, Vol. 2, Mexican Ministry of Foreign Affairs and U.S. Commission on Immigration Reform, Mexico City and Washington D.C., 1998a.

Van Hook, Jennifer, and Frank Bean, "Estimating Underenumeration Among Unauthorized Mexican Migrants to the United States: Applications of Mortality Analysis," in *Migration Between Mexico and the United States, Binational Study*, Vol. 2, Mexican Ministry of Foreign Affairs and U.S. Commission on Immigration Reform, Mexico City and Washington D.C., 1998b.

Vernez, Georges, and Kevin F. McCarthy, *The Cost of Immigration to Tax Payers: Analytical and Policy Issues,* RAND, Santa Monica, California, 1996.

Warren, Robert, "Annual Estimates of Nonimmigrant Overstays in the United States: 1985 to 1988," in Frank D. Bean, Barry Edmonston, and Jeffrey S. Passel (eds.), *Undocumented Migration to the United*

*States: IRCA and the Experience of the 1980s,* Urban Institute Press, Washington, D.C., 1990, pp. 77–110.

Warren, Robert, "Estimates of the Unauthorized Immigrant Population Residing in the United States, by Country of Origin and State of Residence: October 1992," U.S. Immigration and Naturalization Service, Washington, D.C., unpublished report, 1994.

Warren, Robert, *Estimates of the Undocumented Immigrant Population Residing in the United States: October 1996,* U.S. Immigration and Naturalization Service, Washington, D.C., 1997.

Warren, Robert, *Annual Estimates of the Unauthorized Population Residing in the United States and Components of Changes: 1987 to 1997,* U.S. Immigration and Naturalization Service, Washington, D.C., 2000.

Warren, Robert, and Jeffrey S. Passel, "A Count of the Uncountable: Estimates of Undocumented Aliens Counted in the 1980 United States Census," *Demography,* Vol. 24, No. 3, 1987, pp. 375–393.

Woodrow, Karen A., "Preliminary Estimates of Undocumented in 1990; Demographic Analysis Project D2," United States Bureau of the Census, Washington, D.C., Preliminary Research and Evaluation Memorandum No. 75, 1991.

Woodrow, Karen A., "A Consideration of the Effect of Immigration Reform on the Number of Undocumented Residents in the United States," *Population Research and Policy Review,* Vol. 11, 1992, pp. 117–144.

Woodrow, Karen A., "In Search of a Method: Judgment and the Problem of Estimating Unknown Migration," unpublished paper, 1996.

Woodrow, Karen A., and Jeffrey S. Passel, "Post-IRCA Undocumented Immigration to the United States: An Assessment Based on the June 1988 CPS," in Frank D. Bean, Barry Edmonston, and Jeffrey S. Passel (eds.), *Undocumented Migration to the United States: IRCA and the Experience of the 1980s,* Urban Institute Press, Washington, D.C., 1990, pp. 33–76.

Woodrow, Karen A., Jeffrey S. Passel, and Robert Warren, "Preliminary Estimates of Undocumented Immigration to the United States, 1980–1986: Analysis of the June 1986 Current Population Survey,"

*Proceedings of the Social Statistics Section of the American Statistical Association Meeting,* San Francisco, California, 1987.

Word, David L., *The Census Bureau Approach for Allocating Internal Migration to States, Counties and Places: 1981–1991,* Population Estimates and Projections Technical Working Paper Series, Report No. 1, U.S. Bureau of the Census, Washington, D.C., 1992.

Zimmerman, Wendy, "The SAVE Program: An Early Assessment," in Michael Fix (ed.), *The Paper Curtain: Employer Sanctions' Implementation, Impact, and Reform,* Urban Institute Press, Washington, D.C., 1991.

# About the Authors

## BELINDA REYES

Belinda Reyes, a research fellow at the Public Policy Institute of California, studies immigration issues and the economic progress of race and ethnic minorities in California. She has been a senior associate at PolicyLink; a lecturer at the University of California, Berkeley; a research fellow at the University of Michigan; and a visiting scholar at the Federal Reserve Bank of San Francisco. She holds a B.S. in economics from the University of Illinois, Urbana-Champaign, and a Ph.D. in economics from the University of California, Berkeley.

## HANS JOHNSON

Hans Johnson is a demographer whose research interests include international and domestic migration, population estimates and projections, and state and local demography. Before joining PPIC as a research fellow, he was a senior demographer at the California Research Bureau, where he conducted research for the state legislature and the governor's office on population issues. He has also worked as a demographer at the California Department of Finance, specializing in population projections. He holds a Ph.D. in demography from the University of California, Berkeley.

## RICHARD VAN SWEARINGEN

Richard Van Swearingen is a research associate at the Public Policy Institute of California. Before joining PPIC, he performed statistical analyses for the Center for Health Care Evaluation at Stanford University. He holds a B.A. in political science from the University of Texas at Austin, where he also conducted research on the labor market effects of immigration at the Population Research Center.

# Related PPIC Publications

*Falling Behind or Moving Up? The Intergenerational Progress of Mexican Americans*
Jeffrey Grogger, Stephen J. Trejo

*Understanding the Future of California's Fertility: The Role of Immigrants*
Laura E. Hill, Hans P. Johnson

*Undocumented Immigration to California: 1980–1993*
Hans P. Johnson

*Taking the Oath: An Analysis of Naturalization in California and the United States*
Hans P. Johnson, Belinda I. Reyes, Laura Mameesh, and Elisa Barbour

"Trends in Family and Household Poverty"
*California Counts: Population Trends and Profiles*
Volume 1, Number 3, May 2000
Hans P. Johnson and Sonya M. Tafoya

*Dynamics of Immigration: Return Migration to Western Mexico*
Belinda I. Reyes

*Local and Global Networks of Immigrant Professionals in Silicon Valley*
AnnaLee Saxenian

"Check One or More . . . Mixed Race and Ethnicity in California"
*California Counts: Population Trends and Profiles*
Volume 1, Number 2, January 2000
Sonya M. Tafoya

PPIC publications may be ordered by phone or from our website
(800) 232-5343 [mainland U.S.]
(415) 291-4400 [Canada, Hawaii, overseas]
www.ppic.org